RELIGIONS AND ISSUES

CW00421574

Hindu Traditions & Practice

JENNY ROSE

OLIVER & BOYD · OLIVER & BOYD · OLIVER & BOYD · OLIVER & BOYD · OLIVER & BOYD · OLIVER & BOYD · OLIVER & BOYD

Acknowledgements

The author is most grateful to the following people for their help during the preparation of this book:

David G. Bowen, Bob Jackson, Helen Kanitkar, Meg McDonald, D.L. Sharma and Tom Stannage.

The author and publishers are grateful to the following for permission to reproduce copyright photographs:

page 6, Victoria and Albert Museum; page 9, David Richardson, page 11, Hutchison Picture Library/Liba Taylor; page 12, Werner Forman Archive; page 13, Victoria and Albert Museum; page 15, Jenny Rose; page 18, Mark Edwards/Still Pictures; page 19, (left) Mark Edwards/Still Pictures, (right) Vicky White/The Photo Coop; page 20 (left) Ron Giling/Panos Pictures, (right) Mark Edwards/Still Pictures; pp. 22–3, International Society for Krishna Consciousness; page 24, Hutchison Picture Library; page 25 (top) Ron Giling Panos Pictures, (others) Mark Edwards/Still Pictures; page 26, D.L. Sharma; page 29, Sarah Wyld/The Photo Coop; page 30, *The Times*; page 31 (top) Werner Forman Archive, (lower) Victoria and Albert Museum; page 32, Werner Forman Archive, (lower) Vicky White/The Photo Coop; page 37 (top) WHO/ZAFAR; (lower) WHO/M Puhl; page 38, Jenny Rose; page 39, Vicky White/The Photo Coop; page 40, WHO; page 41, Mark Edwards/Still Pictures; page 42 (top) WHO, (lower) Philip Steele/ICCE; page 45, Hutchison Picture Library; page 48, Victoria and Albert Museum.

Illustrations by Cauldron Design Studio and Joanna Stubbs

Oliver & Boyd
Longman House
Burnt Mill
Harlow, Essex CM 20 2JE
An imprint of Longman Group UK Ltd

ISBN 0 05 004488 5
First published 1990

Produced by Longman Group (F.E.) Ltd.
Printed in Hong Kong

Contents

Introduction

Note to teachers and students

Teachers

AIM

This book on Hindu ethics is intended to be studied as part of a GCSE syllabus concerned with ethical issues in world religions. It should not be regarded as a comprehensive introduction to the Hindu religion, nor as a definitive work on Hindu traditions and practices.

CONTENTS

The source materials and texts attempt to provide an overview of the mainstream 'Hindu' position on various ethical issues. Each section has been produced after consultation with a range of Hindu authorities.

HOW TO USE THE BOOK

The book has been designed to meet the assessment objectives of the GCSE syllabus. Teachers will find that pupils are encouraged to use their own powers of inquiry, research and analysis to complete the tasks. The Coursework assignments may be decided through teacher/pupil consultation.

It is assumed that the teacher will have familiarised pupils with the general vocabulary of ethics, and also that both teacher and pupils will be familiar with the basic beliefs of Hinduism before studying Hindu ethics.

The Hindu tradition contains one of the oldest moral philosophies in the history of civilisation. The main sources of Hindu beliefs and practices are the *Vedas* and other *Shastras* (scriptures). The mantras of the Rig Veda contain the concepts of universal moral law (*ṛta*), non-violence (*ahimsa*), the caste-system and the stages of life (*ashramas*). These concepts provide the social setting for the scheme of Hindu ethics.

The different beliefs and practices of Hindus around the world do not detract from the generally-accepted social organisation and its inherent ethical structure. Traditional teachings regarding behaviour towards others is retained, although the approach to certain ethical issues may vary according to the persuasion of the individual, to sectarian bias or to caste allegiance.

It is important to recognise that the terms 'orthodox' and 'heterodox' are applied rather to the teachings and adherents of the various sects, particularly the worshippers of Vishnu and Shiva (the Vaishnavite and Shaivite sects) than to Hinduism as a whole. This book includes quotations from some influential Hindus whose views, although considered 'unorthodox' by some, are nonetheless widely accepted.

Before using this book, the teacher should introduce the students to the following areas of knowledge:

1. The Hindu scriptures (*Shastras*)
   (a) *shruti* (heard): the *Veda Samhitas, Brahmanas* and *Upanishads*
   (b) *smriti* (recollected tradition): *Dharma Shastra* (especially the *Brahma Sutra*)
   (c) *purana* (ancient story): *Ramayana* and *Mahabharata* (including the *Bhagavad Gita*)

DUCTION • INTRODUCTION • INTRODUCTION • INTRODUCTION • INTRODUCTION • INTRODUCTION • INTRODUCTION • INTRODUCTION • INTRO

DUCTION • INTRODUCTION • INTRODUCTION • INTRODUCTION • INTRODUCTION • INTRODUCTION • INTRODUCTION • INTRODUCTION • INTRO

2. The caste system: concepts of *varna, jati, ashrama, dharma.*
3. Philosophical concepts: *karma, samsara, moksha/mukti, atman.*
4. Hindu mythology: the concept of Brahman, God/gods and goddesses, *avatar.*
5. A general understanding of the historical development of Hinduism and the many different traditions it embodies.

RESOURCES

The book itself does not provide detailed resources for information on Hindu traditions and practice. Further research including a deeper study of the Hindu texts themselves and some contact with members of the Hindu community will help pupils to understand more about Hindu life.

Students

AIM

The aim of this book is to look at some contemporary world issues as seen through the eyes of Hindus.

CONTENTS

The beliefs of a religion are found in its daily practices, rites of passage and festivals as well as in its sacred writings. The ethical teachings are found in these beliefs and practices.

This book introduces the main beliefs of Hindus through the 'Sacred Thread' ceremony; through a ritual performed during pregnancy, called 'Seemantonnayana'; and through the festival of 'Divali' or 'Deepavali'.

We then look at five ethical issues from the perspective of these beliefs. The issues appear in this order: 'Work and Wealth'; 'Personal Relationships'; 'Drugs'; 'Peace and Conflict'; 'Relations with other faiths'.

HOW TO USE THIS BOOK

As a reader of this book, you can use the material in a way that suits your own syllabus. You should, however, be familiar with the Introductory section on Hindu beliefs before going on to look at the specific ethical issues.

KEEPING A DICTIONARY

There are words in this book which may not be familiar to you. Many of them will be printed in **dark type**. Start a dictionary or word list to include all of these words, with definitions, and page references from this book. You may have to look in other books for a detailed definition. If you do, be sure to note the source. An alphabetical arrangement may be a useful aid for revision purposes.

HINDU BELIEFS • HINDU BELIEFS • HINDU BELIEFS • HINDU BELIEFS • HINDU BELIEFS • HINDU BELIEFS • HINDU BELIEFS • HINDU BELIEFS •

HINDU BELIEFS • HINDU BELIEFS • HINDU BELIEFS • HINDU BELIEFS • HINDU BELIEFS • HINDU BELIEFS • HINDU BELIEFS • HINDU BELIEFS •

Hindu Beliefs

An Introduction

According to one Hindu writer,

'The basis of Hindu ethics is simple, sensible and logical. The object of a person's life is to renounce the world and merge with God; anything that takes one towards unity with God and away from attachment to and involvement with the world is good . . . . any deed, word or thought that takes one away from God and gets one more and more involved with the world and its mundane material and physical pursuits is bad, unethical. The entire external structure of Hinduism is based on this simple principle and all actions, words and thoughts can be tested on this basis.'
(D.L. Sharma)

Krishna playing the flute

Activities

1. (a) From what you know of Hindu beliefs, what do you think the writer means when he speaks of 'renouncing the world' and 'being attached to the world'? In your own words, define both of these terms.
   (b) Make a list of deeds, words and thoughts that may 'attach' us to the world.
2. Now look at the game of Snakes and Ladders.
   (a) Make a list of the 'snakes' and 'ladders' under the headings: 'Unethical Conduct' and 'Ethical Conduct'.
   (b) Play the game with a partner.

THE HINDU TRADITION

Snakes and Ladders game

This game illustrates the Hindu belief in a series of rebirths leading to the ultimate goal of *moksha*, or release from the cycle of rebirth.

All players begin at space 36. The first player throws two dice or spins a spinner and moves his or her marker ahead according to the sum of the dice or the number on the spinner. If the marker lands on a snake's head, symbolising evil behaviour, it must be moved down to the square at the snake's tail, indicating rebirth in a lower, animal form. If the marker lands at the bottom of a ladder, symbolising virtuous behaviour, it may be advanced to the square at the top of the ladder, thus shortening the soul's journey toward *moksha*. Players follow one another in turn. The object of the game is to see who reaches *moksha* first.

It should be noted that the **atman** does not only move up and down from human ↔ animal, as shown in this game, but also from male ↔ female, **jati** ↔ **jati** and **varna** ↔ **varna**.

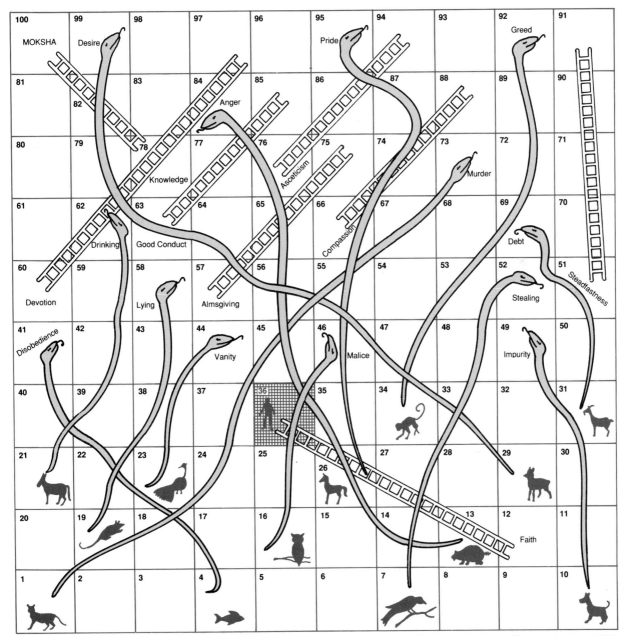

© Copyright Argus Communications 1978.

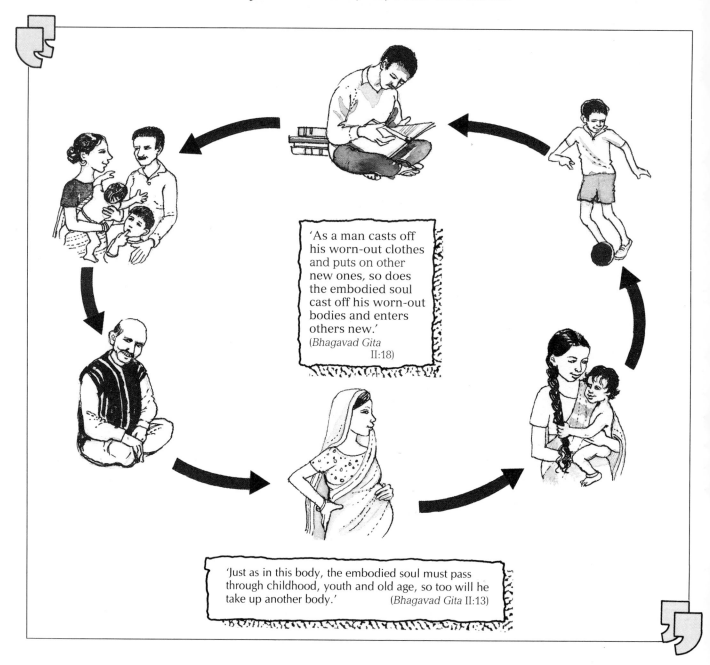

'As a man casts off his worn-out clothes and puts on other new ones, so does the embodied soul cast off his worn-out bodies and enters others new.'
(*Bhagavad Gita* II:18)

'Just as in this body, the embodied soul must pass through childhood, youth and old age, so too will he take up another body.' (*Bhagavad Gita* II:13)

THE 'SACRED THREAD' CEREMONY

For the Hindu, human life is regarded as a journey of growth and development towards a higher spiritual state. To remind the Hindu of this progress, rituals or **samskaras** are performed at various stages of life, beginning with conception and ending with cremation. Of the sixteen samskaras, the 'sacred thread' initiation ceremony is the most important for boys from the top three sections of society or **varnas**.

The ceremony usually takes place when the boy is eight to twelve years old, although sometimes he may be five or younger. After the initiation, he begins a

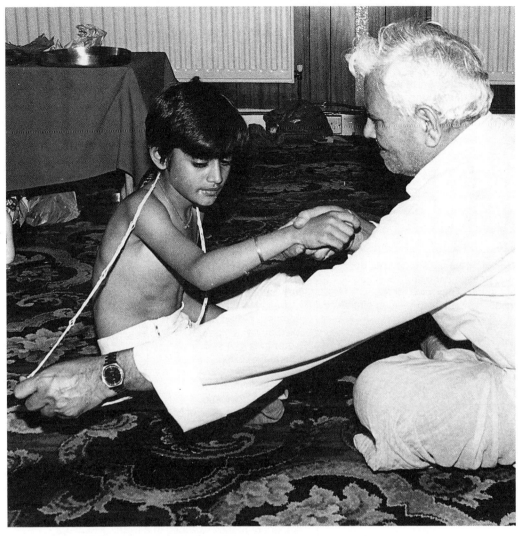

The Sacred
Thread ceremony

period of religious instruction, learning and discussing the Sanskrit scriptures with a **guru** or teacher. Nowadays the ritual is not performed as much, but is still common with Brahmin families. The thread ceremony used to be for girls too, in ancient times, and there is some movement to restore it in India. Girls are allowed to learn Sanskrit, but may not recite the Vedas in public worship.

THE SEEMANTONNAYANA CEREMONY

One of the most popular ceremonies amongst female Hindus in Britain is the **Seemantonnayana**, the 'Hair-parting' ceremony, sometimes called the 'Lap ceremony'. This is the third samskara. The ceremony usually takes place during the seventh month of a woman's first pregnancy, but may occur earlier or later. The rituals of the ceremony vary according to the traditions of each community. The origin of the ritual is Vedic.

The ceremony is a public celebration of the woman's pregnancy, and also helps to reassure the expectant mother that she has the support and care of her family and friends. It shows people that the child will be born into a welcoming, protective environment. The ceremony also sets a pattern for the future religious upbringing of the child. The ceremonies connected with pregnancy all show how important childbirth is considered to be and also emphasise the needs and role of the mother.

THE SEEMANTONNAYANA CEREMONY

1. Close family, friends and other relations are invited to the house in which the ceremony will take place. It usually occurs on a Tuesday or Sunday, both days associated with the **Mata** or mother goddess.

2. The pregnant woman sits on a low stool or sometimes a swinging seat decorated with flowers in front of the family shrine.

3. The husband or a priest or the girl's mother offers prayers to the deities and praises the beauty and good nature of the expectant mother. They wish for the safe delivery of a healthy child. The mother-to-be also offers prayers and thanks.

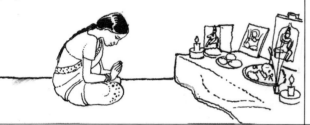

4. Then she bathes, washes her hair and puts on new clothes. Her hair is combed, parted and oiled by her sister or sister-in-law. A strip of material is laid on the floor upon which she walks when she returns. A coin, and a betel nut, symbols of good fortune, are placed in front of her foot at each step.

5. When she is seated again, she is anointed with oils and perfumes by the other women, who put fresh flowers in her hair. These other women, who are usually also married, will assist the pregnant woman in the time before and after her delivery.

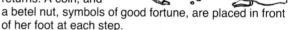

6. A married woman, who has successfully given birth and who has had no miscarriages or abortions, offers rice, coconut, green moong (bean shoots), betel nut and a small amount of money wrapped in a cloth. These are passed to the lap of the pregnant woman. They are said to bring 'goodness and good fortune' to the woman.

7. The husband's sister then places a silver protective bangle on the woman's wrist, wishing her a safe and easy delivery. Sometimes, a small baby of five or six months old is placed in the woman's lap, symbolically enacting the birth of her own child.

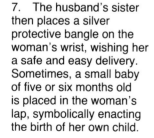

8. Many different dishes of food have been prepared and the mother-to-be is encouraged to eat a mouthful of each dish. All the guests are then served refreshments.

1. Look carefully at the pictures in the circle and the verses on page 8. Make sure that you understand the Hindu concept of **reincarnation**. Now, write your own verse or draw a picture which includes all the relevant ideas connected with this concept.
2. (a) Write an 'eye-witness' account of the main events of the Seemantonnayana ceremony, as if you were one of the women present.
   (b) Think about the importance of this ceremony for:
      i) The expectant mother;
      ii) the unborn child;
      iii) the Hindu community.
   Write down your thoughts.

(c) Why do you think such a fuss is made of an expectant mother, particularly during her first pregnancy? Discuss this with your neighbour.
(d) If you had a child, what five things would you wish for it at birth? (For example, good health.) Draw a gift card to illustrate these wishes.
3. Begin your dictionary of important words and phrases. Look up these words and write down brief definitions of each of them:

MOKSHA	VARNA	REINCARNATION
SAMSKARA	SAMSARA	GURU
BRAHMIN	VEDAS	MATA

A HINDU FESTIVAL: DIVALI

There are many different times of celebration within the Hindu tradition. Some of these, such as Seemantonnayana, mark an important event or time in someone's life; others remember significant events in the long history of the Indian people and their gods and goddesses. Festivals are important for the Hindu children's awareness of their religious tradition. They enjoy participating in the celebrations and eating the special foods. Indian movies often have scenes showing the celebration of various festivals.

Divali, also known as Deepavali ('line of lights'), is one of the most popular Hindu festivals. It takes place soon after the monsoon and is celebrated in different ways throughout India and the rest of the world, since it is associated with different events within the Hindu tradition. The theme of good overcoming evil, symbolised by the lighting of lamps, is common to all Divali celebrations. Most Hindus clean and decorate their homes in preparation for this festival, which lasts about five days, beginning at the end of the month of Ashvin (October/November).

The first day

On the evening of the first day of the festival, one or more lamps with a single flame are placed on the south side of the house, in honour of **Yama**, the God of Death.

Here is a **diva**. The word 'diva' or 'deepa' means 'lamp'.

The second day

Below is an account of the morning of the second day of Divali.

'Something went off with an explosive bang. It was half-past four in the morning, and still very dark. It wouldn't be dawn for an hour or more. The birds were still asleep in the trees, and the violent noise didn't seem to have disturbed them, but they would commence their quarrelsome chatter just as soon as it began to get light. There was a slight ground mist, but the stars were very clear. After the first explosion, several others followed in the distance; there was a period of quiet, and then fireworks began going off all over the place. The festive day had begun. That morning, the birds didn't carry on with their chatter as long as usual, but cut it short and rapidly scattered, for those violent sounds were frightening; but towards evening they would assemble again in the same trees, to tell each other noisily of their daily doings. The sun was now touching the tree-tops, and they were aglow with soft light; lovely in their quietude, they were giving shape to the sky. The single rose in the garden was heavy with dew. Though it was already noisy with fireworks, the town was slow and leisurely about waking up, for it was one of the great holidays of the year; there would be feasting and rejoicing, and both rich and poor would be giving things to each other.

As it grew dark that evening, the people began to assemble on the banks of the river. They were gently setting afloat on the water small, burnt-clay saucers full of oil, with a wick burning. They would say a prayer and let the lights go floating off down the river. Soon there were thousands of these points of light on the dark, still water. It was an astonishing sight to behold, the eager faces lit by the little flames, and the river a miracle of light. The heavens with their myriad stars looked down on this river of light, and the earth was silent with the love of the people.'

(J. Krishnamurti)

It is usual to tell the story of how Krishna defeated the demon Narakasura on this day.

The legend of Narakasura

'Narakasura was a fearsome demon (or a tyrant king!) in the country of Pragjyotisha, which some authorities identify with the western portion of modern Assam. He carried off the daughter of Vishwa-Karma, the architect of the Gods. The demon was a notorious kidnapper of girls and had carried off 16 000 young women. Now that he had carried off a celestial damsel, something had to be done. No woman felt safe either on Earth or in Heaven. The women of the upper and lower world joined together and appealed to Vishnu to destroy Narakasura and restore the sanctity of female honour. Narakasura was a pious demon who had performed penance and meditation and accumulated spiritual merit. For a time his spiritual merit outweighed his bad deeds, but as time went on, his sins outweighed the merit and so Vishnu asked Krishna to destroy the demon. Narakasura was granted one boon because of his spiritual merit before he was killed. The demon said, "Let this day be commemorated as a day of feasting in the world." "So be it," said Krishna, before he struck the blow with his sword. The story is told to illustrate that no one is totally bad and even a small good deed will be remembered. The 16 000 women were released, and they immediately considered Krishna their Lord and Master, hence the legend that Krishna had 16 000 wives.*'

(V.P. Kanitkar)

(*According to Hindu tradition, Krishna legally and religiously married all of the women.)

12

The third day

The third day of Divali is dedicated to **Laxmi**, the goddess of prosperity. On this day, **rangoli** patterns are drawn on the floor near the entrance to the house. There is often a drawing of a lotus flower, since this is said to be the favourite sitting-place of the goddess. Many oil lamps are placed in the window of the house to welcome Laxmi. This is traditionally the day on which bankers and business people close one financial year and begin the new one by opening new accounts and entering into new contracts. Business account books are ceremonially blessed in the temple, in the hope that the new year will be a prosperous one.

The fifth day

The fifth day of Divali is celebrated as Sisters' Day, (sometimes called Brothers' Day). Usually brothers do not visit sisters in their home or accept anything from them, but on this day it is the sister's privilege to invite her brothers to her house and to offer them food and presents. Men are therefore supposed to visit their sister's home, where they are welcomed with sugar. The sister will anoint her brother with perfumed oil on his head, arms and back and then puts a dot of **kumkum** (red powder) on his forehead. She will present a lamp in front of him, moving it in a circle to ward off evil. He will give her a present and after sharing a midday meal with her and her family, will return home.

'The festival of Divali combines legends, wealth, new undertakings and social and family obligations. It is a joyous occasion and there should be light in every heart as there is light everywhere else.'

(V.P. Kanitkar)

Activities

1. Read the section on Divali.
   (a) What does the name 'Divali' or 'Deepavali' mean?
   (b) What do the lights symbolise during this festival?
   (c) Can you think of 'festivals of light' in any other religions? Compare what you know of these festivals with Divali.
2. Here is a traditional rangoli pattern. Using the legends and events connected with the festival of Divali, make your own rangoli pattern with coloured chalks or paper to illustrate one of these ideas: family; prosperity; light; good versus evil.

   A rangoli pattern

3. From the passages throughout this introductory section, choose some that show the traditional Hindu attitude to the following issues: a) wealth; b) women; c) family relations.
   Carefully write out the sentences which relate to each of those headings, and briefly explain what you learn from them.
4. *Further Research*
   Laxmi is the consort of the God **Vishnu**.
   (a) From your library, find out all you can about her and her role as a Hindu goddess.
   (b) What are the other female deities?
   (c) What is their role in family or community worship?
   (d) How important is the idea of the **Mata** within the Hindu tradition?
5. Add these new words to your dictionary.

DIVALI/DEEPAVALI	LAXMI	KRISHNA
KUMKUM	YAMA	RANGOLI

Work and Wealth

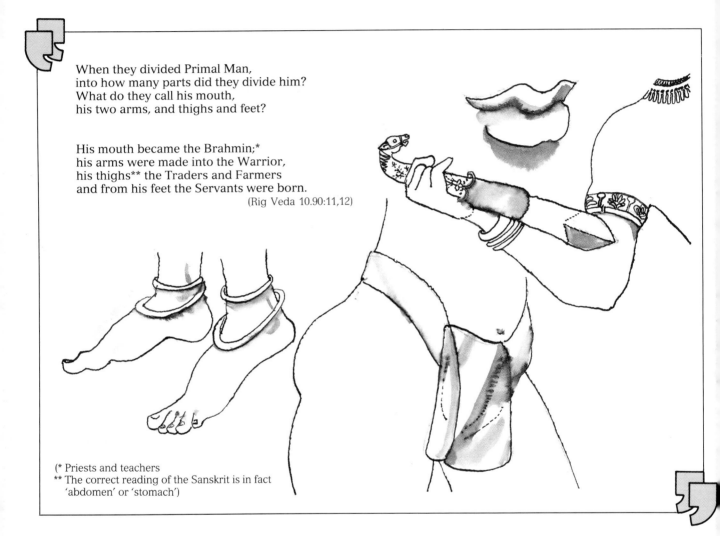

When they divided Primal Man,
into how many parts did they divide him?
What do they call his mouth,
his two arms, and thighs and feet?

His mouth became the Brahmin;*
his arms were made into the Warrior,
his thighs** the Traders and Farmers
and from his feet the Servants were born.
(Rig Veda 10.90:11,12)

(* Priests and teachers
** The correct reading of the Sanskrit is in fact
'abdomen' or 'stomach')

WORK

Traditionally, the profession of each Hindu was linked with his or her social position (**varna**). The caste system was one way in which the social order was maintained; it controlled the relationships and responsibilities of groups and individuals. One's **jati**, birth into a certain caste, shaped the individual's awareness of his or her role and purpose in life. The ancient term **varnashramadharma** refers to the moral obligation (**dharma**) of each Hindu to follow caste duty (**varna**) and to fulfil the requirements of each stage of life (**ashrama**).

Caste duty

The priestly caste, the **Brahmin**, was the highest social category to which traditionally, priests, law-givers, teachers, administrators and intellectuals belonged. In Vedic times, they had the greatest religious responsibility – to learn and teach Sanskrit and to perform Vedic ritual. It was also common for the cooks at community festivals to be Brahmins, since all classes could accept food from the Brahmins without fear of being 'polluted' through contact with the lower castes. There are still many Brahmins in domestic service as cooks today. Nowadays, many professional people are from the Brahmin class, since a good education was always recognised as important for both Brahmin girls and boys. Many became soldiers in the time of the Raj, or entered the Government, since they were well-educated.

A Brahmin priest

The **Kshatriya**, the second caste, were the aristocracy who ruled in both a military and a political way. Their main role was to protect society in times of war and to govern well in times of peace.

Many British Hindus belong to the third caste, the **Vaishya**, although there are of course Brahmins, Kshatriya and Shudra as well. The Vaishya group is connected with trading; often they are merchants or shopkeepers, but the class also includes skilled workers, different kinds of craftworkers and agriculturalists.

The fourth caste is the **Shudra**. These are the artisans – servants, farm labourers and service castes, such as sweepers, barbers and launderers. Their job, according to the shastras, is to look after and serve the other three castes.

It is important to realise, however, that both economic and social changes have caused certain groups to abandon their traditional family occupations. With the introduction of new jobs such as computer programming, the traditional division of labour according to class is less applicable.

Sometimes included in the fourth caste, but usually regarded as 'outcastes', are the **Harijans**. Mahatma Gandhi gave them the title 'harijan', which means 'people of God'. Some people still refer to this group as the Untouchables or pariahs. They do work considered to be too polluting for the higher castes. This work includes the brewing of alcohol, leatherwork, midwifery and the disposal of the bodies of dead animals.

Although the caste system has officially been abolished in India and the Untouchability (Offences) Act was passed in the Indian Parliament in 1955, giving fundamental rights to the Harijans, there is still local prejudice against harijans holding certain jobs.

'VILLAGE VOICE'

CASTE ASIDE

by VICTOR ZORZA

Government officials combed the whole area for a youth who could read and write well, was articulate, and had other rare skills. They picked Vijay, then in his teens, because they recognised him as the potential leader they were looking for. He was sent to boarding school.

After a few years he went on to the city where he lived with others as an equal – an amazing experience for someone brought up in a village as a Harijan, an Untouchable. He could find lodgings everywhere, instead of being confined to a Harijan colony. When the heat made him thirsty, he could drink from water-fountains the Government had made accessible to all – regardless of caste. He ate at the same table as high caste townspeople.

Vijay set up a school in a distant village, where high-caste hostility to an untouchable 'guru' might be less. At first the Rajputs were glad that their children were learning to read and write. Then they decided that the risk was too great. Their children, instead of commanding an Untouchable, would learn to obey him. Vijay was asked to leave, politely. When he refused, the Rajputs besieged the school house for four days, stoned him whenever he came out and finally drove him away.

(Taken from an article by Victor Zorza, *The Guardian*, 18 April 1982)

The four ashramas

Apart from the traditional occupation which is related to one's status in the social order, the Hindu also has certain functions to fulfil at different stages in his or her life. There are four main stages or **ashramas**, which each have their own moral and social obligations, although these are not now so strictly observed. The ashramas apply to any individual of whatever class or caste, and represent a way that the individual may choose to realise God. Traditionally, each ashrama is supposed to last twenty-five years since it is believed that if one conducted oneself properly, one should be able to live to the age of a hundred.

The four ashramas

Brahmacharya – studentship. Usually this ashrama lasts only twelve to fifteen years. This is the period of preparation for a mature and useful adult life and is the time of formal education, not only for a future profession, but for family life, social responsibilities and religious duties. The student is supposed to live a chaste, morally-disciplined life.

Grihasthya – the householder stage. During this period, the Hindu is supposed to get married, devote time and energy to raising a family, earning a living and contributing to the welfare of the community. This stage now usually lasts well beyond the age of fifty, since most people are reluctant to give up material pleasures and their family life as demanded by the third and fourth ashramas.

Vanaprastha – the forest dweller stage. The shastras recommend that after reaching the age of fifty, a person should retire from family life, professional work, wealth, possessions and position. A man hands over the family responsibility to his sons and retreats into a forest, or at least away from the family, to spend time in meditation and preparation for the next existence.

Sannyasi – the homeless wanderer stage. After the age of 75, the Hindu is expected to break all ties with family, home and friends in preparation for renouncing the world and merging with God. This is the Hindu ideal. To the family, the sannyasi is now regarded as non-existent, or as dead. He or she now relies on charity for food and other needs. Very few people are able to follow the third and fourth ashramas.

Dharma

Dharma is usually translated as 'moral duty' or 'moral law'. The Hindu tradition itself is referred to as **Sanatan Dharma**, 'the eternal moral law'. Dharma is the correct conduct for the four varnas and the four ashramas. It is one of the acceptable aims of life, which a Hindu should work towards. Through following one's dharma, the Hindu is said to achieve a balanced approach to physical, material and spiritual existence. Insofar as it concerns an individual's life-pattern, dharma may be translated as 'moral righteousness'.

Detachment from work

According to traditional Hindu thought, the word for 'work', **karma**, means any action or activity. All actions are said to have results of some kind. As one Hindu says:

'Each single act can affect the whole personality, however slightly. Thus a single karma (activity) of being angry will have many effects on the person concerned. One result could be that the next time he would be able to exercise better control over himself. Or the effect could be quite the reverse, and next time he might get angry more easily. In any case, the karma will affect the personality. At the time of death, the essence of that personality will pass on to one's next life.'
(D.L. Sharma)

Correct behaviour is therefore very important both in one's place of work and in one's ethical conduct, but ideally one should not become too involved with any activity. Hinduism teaches that you should perform your duty according to your caste and according to your stage of life, but in a detached way so that you do not desire to gain from them or achieve anything by them. It is only this complete detachment that will free you from your actions (karma).

'When all a man's undertakings
Have neither motive nor desire
His works burnt up in wisdom's fire
Then wise men call him learned.

When he's cast off all attachment
to the fruit of works,
Ever-content, on none dependent,
Though he embarks on work,
In fact, he does no work at all.

Nothing hoping, his thought and mind restrained,
Giving up all possessions,
He only does such work
As is needed for the body's maintenance,
And so avoids defilement.'
(*Bhagavad Gita* 4:19–21)

One writer explains this teaching concerning detachment from work; here, 'work' means one's professional job, household or family duties or any other action that one does.

> *'To act without attachment to the fruits of an act is to act without fear or desire; desire that a certain result may be obtained, fear that it may not – or vice versa, when it is a question of doing one's duty in the face of possibly unpleasant consequences. We are to perform every action as though it were a ritual, of which the value is symbolic. We perform this ritual to the very best of our ability, but without anxiety as to what its consequences may be. The consequences – the 'fruits' of the act – we dedicate to God.'* (C. Isherwood, *Ramakrishna*)

Satyagraha

This is another important concept connected with the Hindu approach to work. It means 'firmness in truth'. According to Mahatma Gandhi, it is this concept that is the basis for all ethical action. He said that in order to act correctly in any situation, the **Satyagrahi** (the one who practises Satyagraha) must see the truth of that situation and recognise the evil in it. Truth can only be seen if the mind is loving and free from hatred and prejudice. Once truth is discovered, then action must follow. According to Gandhi, the action must always be non-violent.

Non-violent non-cooperation

Although Mahatma Gandhi was basically a peaceful man, he was concerned about the welfare of the Indian people when they were still under British rule. He advised his followers to show that they disagreed with some of the British civil laws in a non-violent way by not co-operating with the government.

Gandhi did not agree with the idea of striking in a place of work, and believed that negotiation should take place between workers and employers wherever possible. In one case, however, he realised that he could not prevent a strike by the mill-workers of Ahmedabad, whose wages were very low. He drew up the following list of recommendations for a successful strike:

1. Never resort to violence
2. Never molest strikebreakers
3. Never depend on alms
4. Remain firm, no matter how long the strike continues, and earn bread during the strike by any other honest labour.

Women and work

In India, as in many other countries, most of the work related to the preparation of meals, cleaning of the dwelling and caring for children is done by women. Whether a Hindu woman also has a career or not depends on her level of education, social status and family expectations.

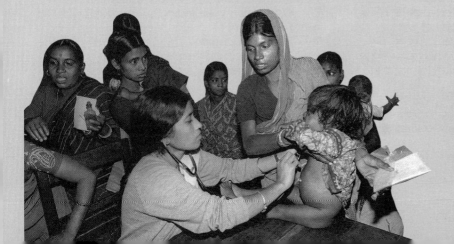

Many women with a good education become doctors, lawyers, or teachers, or go into business. Women doctors are particularly important because of traditional concepts of modesty which frown upon a woman being physically examined by a male doctor. There are therefore many qualified female general practitioners who specialise in gynaecology and obstetrics.

Women with little or no education often belong to the poorer families and have to go out to work to earn money to support their family. Their jobs are usually 'service' work, which may include sweeping someone else's house, or doing their washing of pots and clothes (some do heavier work such as on building sites or in the fields). These are considered by some to be degrading chores. It is a sign of high social status to be able to employ a servant.

One poor widow, employed in such domestic service said:

> All my daughters are studying. After being in my unfortunate position, I know that to get a decent job you must be educated. If I had been better qualified, I might have been able to get a good job and look after my children better. I want them to have a better life than I did.
>
> (quoted in U. Sharma)

Activities

1. (a) In your own words, summarise the work traditionally assigned to the four varnas.
   (b) Now think about how those traditional roles have changed in recent years. Briefly mention those changes and try to explain what may have caused them.
   (c) The passages in this section refer to certain jobs that are 'polluting'. Make a list of these. Think about why they may be considered to be polluting. What jobs have a similar low status in Britain?
   (d) With your neighbour discuss whether there is a division of society and labour in Britain.
2. Draw four pictures to illustrate the duties of a Hindu in the four stages (ashramas) of life.
3. Read again the verses from the *Bhagavad Gita* about 'detachment from work'. Now write a verse of your own to show that you have understood the meaning of the word 'karma'.

Research
1. (a) Read local and national newspapers for a fortnight and cut out anything about workers' conditions or strikes.
   (b) From your knowledge of trades' unions and employers in Britain, do you think that Gandhi's four recommendations for a successful strike would work there? Discuss each point in turn, trying to relate them to particular instances that you have read about. (e.g. should those who have been on strike for a long time accept charity to support their family?).
   (c) Devise a short scene in which 'non-violent non-cooperation' is an effective form of civil disobedience. Either write down the script or enact and record the scene.
2. (a) Conduct a class survey to find out what roles men and women play in most households.
   (b) Write down your findings (this could be in the form of a graph).
   (c) Think about your own education. List the ways in which it will help you to have a reasonable standard of living and a sense of fulfilment in the future.

Dictionary words

KARMA	SATYAGRAHA/SATYAGRAHI
VARNASHRAMADHARMA	
JATI	ASHRAMA DHARMA

WEALTH

The Sanskrit word meaning 'prosperity' or 'wealth' is **artha**. It is one of the four acceptable aims of a Hindu's life. The other three are Kama, sensual pleasure, Dharma, see page 18, and Moksha, release or liberation. A Hindu is not expected to deny himself or his family the good things of life, but is not supposed to become obsessed with acquiring material possessions.

It is easy for people in today's world to become deluded by wealth, thinking that the comforts and luxuries of this world are the only important things. The Upanishads teach, however,

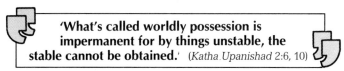

> **'What's called worldly possession is impermanent for by things unstable, the stable cannot be obtained.'** (*Katha Upanishad* 2:6, 10)

and the Rig Veda says;

> *'Let the rich person satisfy the poor beggar,*
> *and bend his eye upon a longer pathway.*
> *Riches come now to one, now to another, and like*
> *the wheels of chariots, are ever moving.'*
> (*Rig Veda* X:117)

Here is what one writer from the Hindu tradition says about those who have a mistaken attitude towards wealth:

> 'The rich have a peculiar atmosphere of their own. They are not the possessors of wealth, but are possessed by wealth, which is worse than death . . . they think they are trustees of their wealth; they have charities, create endowments; they are the makers, the builders, the givers. They build churches, temples, but their god is the god of their gold. With so much poverty and degradation, one must have a very thick skin to be rich. Some of them come to question, to argue, to find reality. For the rich as for the poor, it is extremely difficult to find reality. The poor crave to be rich and powerful, and the rich are already caught in the net of their own action . . .'
> (J. Krishnamurti)

Charity

Unlike certain other religions, there is no compulsory charity in the Hindu tradition, although the duty of almsgiving is mentioned in the *Rig Veda*. Instead of being compelled to give a percentage of the weekly earnings to charity, the individual Hindu has to decide when, how much and to whom to give. It is customary for devout Hindus to divide their earnings into three portions. They will save one third, give one third to charity and live on the remaining third. The shastras place two kinds of charity higher than all others:
(1) the giving of food, or money to buy food;
(2) the provision of education.

Education is thought to be important because of the old saying, 'A hungry person fed today must be fed again tomorrow, but give a person knowledge and he or she can feed themselves and help others for all time.' Also, neither food nor education are gifts which could lead to misuse.

Although there are no worldwide Hindu charities, there are local organised charitable foundations in certain areas of India, such as Gujarat, which help to fund hospitals and hostels.

According to Hindu teaching, there are three basic types, or **gunas**, of human nature: Goodness, Passion and Darkness. Each person's actions correspond to one of these types and this includes even the motives for giving charity.

'Alms given because to give alms is a sacred duty
To one from whom no favour is expected in return
At the right place and time and to a fit recipient –
This is called alms given in Goodness' way.

But alms given in expectation of favours in return
Or for the sake of fruits to be reaped hereafter,
Alms given reluctantly –
This is called alms given in Passion's way.

Alms given at the wrong place and time
To unworthy recipients
Without respect, contemptuously,
This is called in Darkness' way.'

(Bhagavad Gita 17:20–22)

The following text is an enlargement of the ISKCON leaflet on page 23.

Food for life is a division of ISKCON* which distributes free food to those in need. Hunger has often been thought of solely as a Third World problem. Mention faraway places like Ethiopia or Bangladesh and immediately the mind conjures up haunting images of the homeless, ragclad mother with her gaunt malnourished child clutched in her skinny arms.

Recently, however, Americans have been shocked by the startling statistics of increased homelessness and poverty in our very own country. Hunger in the United States has dramatically increased nearly 400 percent in the last decade, and New York City alone, with all its posh condominiums has almost 40 000 homeless people, one of the most staggering statistics in the nation.

FOOD FOR LIFE is ISKCON's humble but ambitious food distribution project that is tackling New York's hunger problem head on. Besides distributing free hot meals to the needy in the Lower East Side, F.F.L. accepts donated foodstuffs which it redistributes to bonafide charitable organizations for use in shelters, senior citizen homes, drug rehabilitation centers, etc.

Above and beyond feeding the needy, F.F.L. goes one step further by educating people (through its mass distribution of literature) in how to prepare wholesome vegetarian meals themselves, simply and cheaply.

Remember, a hungry man fed today, must be fed again tomorrow – but give a man knowledge, and he can help himself and others for all time. So, in addition to feeding people through its FOOD FOR LIFE programs, ISKCON is deeply committed to the printing and distribution of self-help books on transcendental knowledge and vegetarian diet.

Why vegetarianism? Because it happens to be the most economical and nutritious diet known to man. Harvard nutritionist Jean Mayer estimates that reducing meat production by just 10% would release enough grain to feed 60 million people. A United Nations representative recently said that the meat consumption of the rich countries is a key cause of the hunger around the world. Accordingly, the U.N. has recently recommended that these countries cut down on the meat consumption as a genuine step toward helping their fellow men and women. F.F.L. wishes to support this endeavor around the world.

HUNGER IS A PROBLEM

WHO ARE THE HUNGRY?

• There has been a 66% increase in the number of poor New Yorkers since 1970
• More than 1,700,000 New York City residents live below the poverty level
• Almost 40% of all New York City children live in poverty
• Nearly 19% of all New Yorkers over the age of 65 live below the poverty level

These families and individuals cannot afford to buy adequate, nutritious food on a consistent basis. Despite these startling figures, a large number of individuals and families living in poverty do not receive the government benefits to which they are entitled.

HARE KRISHNA
Food for Life

IS THE SOLUTION

Activities

1. Re-read the information about the goddess Laxmi in the introductory section on Divali.

   (a) Using quotes from there and this section, summarise the Hindu attitude to wealth and material possessions.

   (b) With your neighbour, discuss what Krishnamurti means when he talks of someone being 'possessed by wealth'. Write down your ideas.

   (c) Do you think he is right when he says, 'With so much poverty and degradation, one must have a very thick skin to be rich'?

   (d) In your own words, write down what you think the term 'inward poverty' means.

   (e) Choose one of the quotations on the rich and poor from page 21. Write a short poem about the ideas and pictures that it raises in your mind.

2. (a) Read the passage from the *Bhagavad Gita* about almsgiving. Now make up a short dialogue or draw a cartoon to show that you have understood the three different ways of giving charity to another person.

   (b) 'A hungry person fed today must be fed again tomorrow, but give a person knowledge and he or she can feed themselves and help others for all time.'

   Explain what this means.

3. (a) With your neighbour, think about how your 'good' and 'bad' karma may affect your own personality and the lives of others, now and in the future.

   (b) In two columns, make a list of your own activities which might fall under the headings 'Good Karma' and 'Bad Karma'.

   (c) Now write a short story from a Hindu point of view, explaining the possible effects of the karma of greed or miserliness.

   Research

   The Hindu tradition regards vegetarianism as the best form of diet.

   (a) Find out more about the scriptural basis and spiritual significance of this belief.

   (b) Write to Hindu organisations such as ISKCON for further information.

   (c) Compile two daily vegetarian diets which are nutritionally balanced, but inexpensive; one is for a Hindu family living in India, the other for a non-Hindu family living in Great Britain.

   (d) What benefits might arise for humans and animals if more people adopted such a diet?

   (e) Compare the cost of your vegetarian diets with a nutritionally similar meat-based diet. Which is more expensive? Why is this so?

   Dictionary words

ARTHA	ALMS	GUNA	VEGETARIAN

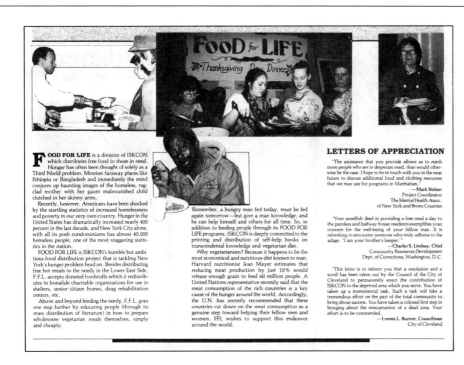

FOOD FOR LIFE is a division of ISKCON which distributes free food to those in need.

Hunger has often been thought of solely as a Third World problem. Mention faraway places like Ethiopia or Bangladesh and immediately the mind conjures up haunting images of the homeless, rag-clad mother with her gaunt malnourished child clutched in her skinny arms.

Recently, however, Americans have been shocked by the startling statistics of increased homelessness and poverty in our very own country. Hunger in the United States has dramatically increased nearly 400 percent in the last decade, and New York City alone, with all its posh condominiums has almost 40,000 homeless people, one of the most staggering statistics in the nation.

FOOD FOR LIFE is ISKCON's humble but ambitious food distribution project that is tackling New York's hunger problem head on. Besides distributing free hot meals to the needy in the Lower East Side, F.F.L. accepts donated foodstuffs which it redistributes to bonafide charitable organizations for use in shelters, senior citizen homes, drug rehabilitation centers, etc.

Above and beyond feeding the needy, F.F.L. goes one step further by educating people (through its mass distribution of literature) in how to prepare wholesome vegetarian meals themselves, simply and cheaply.

Remember, a hungry man fed today, must be fed again tomorrow—but give a man knowledge, and he can help himself and others for all time. So, in addition to feeding people through its FOOD FOR LIFE programs, ISKCON is deeply committed to the printing and distribution of self-help books on transcendental knowledge and vegetarian diet.

Why vegetarianism? Because it happens to be the most economical and nutritious diet known to man. Harvard nutritionist Jean Mayer estimates that reducing meat production by just 10% would release enough grain to feed 60 million people. A United Nations representative recently said that the meat consumption of the rich countries is a key cause of the hunger around the world. Accordingly, the U.N. has recently recommended that these countries cut down on the meat consumption as a genuine step toward helping their fellow men and women, FFL wishes to support this endeavor around the world.

LETTERS OF APPRECIATION

"The assistance that you provide allows us to reach more people who are in desperate need, than would otherwise be the case. I hope to be in touch with you in the near future to discuss additional food and clothing resources that we may use for programs in Manhattan."
—Mark Steiner
Project Coordinator
The Mental Health Assoc.
of New York and Bronx Counties

"Your unselfish deed in providing a free meal a day to the parolees and halfway house residents exemplifies your concern for the well-being of your fellow man. It is refreshing to encounter someone who truly adheres to the adage, 'I am your brother's keeper.'"
—Charles S. Lindsay, Chief
Community Resources Development
Dept. of Corrections, Washington, D.C.

"This letter is to inform you that a resolution and a scroll has been taken out by the Council of the City of Cleveland to permanently enact the contribution of ISKCON to the deprived area which you serve. You have taken up a monumental task. Such a task will take a tremendous effort on the part of the total community to bring about success. You have taken a colossal first step in bringing about the reincarnation of a dead area. Your effort is to be commended."
—Lonnie L. Burton, Councilman
City of Cleveland

*ISKCON stands for International Society for Krishna Consciousness. It began in the 1960s. Most of its members are non-Indians.

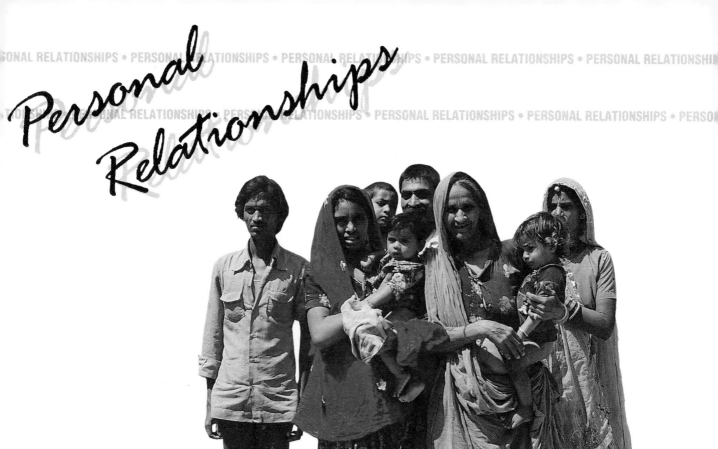

THE FAMILY

The family is the basis of Hindu society. It is through the individual's performance of his or her family duties that moral, social and cosmic order is maintained, although the ideal remains to renounce the world.

In the *Bhagavad Gita*, Arjuna in his ignorance, states

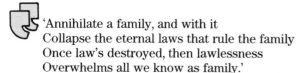

> 'Annihilate a family, and with it
> Collapse the eternal laws that rule the family
> Once law's destroyed, then lawlessness
> Overwhelms all we know as family.'
>
> (*Bhagavad Gita* 1:40)

As we have seen, this is a common conception, and very few people are willing to renounce their families in order to follow the third and fourth ashramas. (See page 17.)

The ideal Hindu man

The ideal role of the Hindu 'family man' is spoken of in these terms in the shastras:

'Having risen before dawn, the Householder should ponder over what is good for the Self. He should not, as far as possible, neglect his duties in respect of the three goals of mankind, namely, virtue (dharma), material gain (artha) and pleasure (kama), at their proper times . . . Learning, religious practice, age, family relations, and wealth, on account of these and in the order mentioned are men honoured in society. By means of these, if possessed in great quantity, even a shudra deserves respect in old age.' (from *Yajnavalkya Smriti* 1:97–116)

The duties of a man towards women in the various stages of his life include:
1. as a husband, providing for his wife's needs both materially and sexually;
2. as a father, ensuring that his daughters are well-married;
3. as a son, looking after his mother on the death of his father.

The duties of a man towards his father are most important at the funeral rituals of the father. The son is obliged to perform the funeral rituals correctly in order to ensure the future of his deceased father's soul. The birth of a male child is, therefore, particularly welcome, since it is necessary for every Hindu male (apart from monks) to have a lawful son who can perform the necessary offerings after his death. If a man does not have a son, he may adopt one who is able to perform the rituals. Sons are also important as an economic asset; in many families, the son continues the traditional profession of the family and stays at home, whereas the daughter marries and leaves the family home for that of her husband.

The ideal Hindu woman

The shastras are inconsistent in their attitude towards women. On the one hand, women are praised as wives and mothers, but on the other hand, they are spoken of as temptresses, whose only aim is to seduce men away from a chaste life. Below are some quotations from the shastras showing these various approaches to women. Read these and write down your own definition of the ideal Hindu woman.

'Between wives who are destined to bear children, who secure many blessings, who are worthy of worship and irradiate their dwellings, and between the goddesses of fortune who reside in the houses of humans, there is no difference whatsoever.' (Manu Smriti)

'. . . The Scriptures teach that the mother has been given a place in the family higher than that of the father, and that she should be shown greater respect and that her wishes are to be carried out in preference to the father's. Traditionally, although Hindu women, as daughters, wives or mothers, receive affection, regard, care and adoration in ample measure; they are not considered suitable for taking on responsibilities, making decisions, shouldering power, discharging public duties or controlling family affairs. Their place has been confined to the home as housewives and mothers . . . .' (D.L. Sharma)

'The production of children, the nurture of those born, and the daily life of men, of these matters woman is visibly the cause.' (Manu Smriti)

'Day and night must women be kept in dependence by the males of their families . . . Her father protects her in childhood, her husband protects her in youth, and her sons protect her in old age; a woman is never fit for independence.' (Manu Smriti)

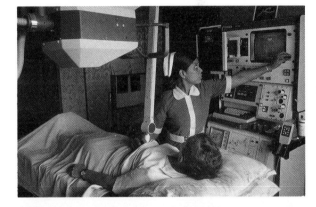

CHOOSING A PARTNER

The Vedic ideal of a relationship is the marriage of a man and a woman who will have mutual respect for each other. This ideal is reflected in the story of Rama and Sita, found in the Hindu epic called the *Ramayana*.

Most Hindus are monogamous, although under certain circumstances, such as the wife's infertility or illness, it is allowed under Hindu law for a man to take another wife. This is not now frequent nor legal according to Indian law. Nowadays, child marriage is forbidden according to Indian law. The Child Marriage Restraint Act of 1929 made marriages of boys under eighteen and girls under fourteen illegal. Mahatma Gandhi describes here his own attitude to child marriage, which echoes the feelings of most modern Hindus:

> 'It is my painful duty to record here my marriage at the age of thirteen. As I see the youngsters of the same age about me who are under my care, and think of my own marriage, I am inclined to pity myself and to congratulate them on having escaped my lot. I can see no moral argument in support of such a preposterously early marriage.'

It should be noted that, as in Gandhi's case, an early marriage did not normally involve cohabitation until a few years later.

An arranged marriage

Since the marriage rite is thought of as an eternal bond, it is felt necessary to find an appropriate partner. Below is an interview with a Hindu grandfather who arranged the marriage of his son.

Q: How did you set about finding a suitable wife for your son?

Mr Sharma: There are various criteria for choosing the partner. I based my decision on the reading of the astrological charts, caste, education, family background and physical appearance of several girls.

Q: How important is the use of astrological charts?

Mr Sharma: The use of astrology dates back to the time of the Puranas (ancient stories). Nowadays, an individual's chart is usually written at about three to four years' old. It defines the person's character and predicts the future, covering such areas as wealth and property, education, the number of children, relationship with the government or civil authorities, relationship with parents and one's religious awareness.

An astrological chart

Q: Is the partner chosen from the same caste?

Mr Sharma: Often the marriage partner is selected from a nearby family of the same caste. One cannot marry cousins, or members of the families of one's father, mother's father, or paternal and maternal grandmother's father. It is preferred if the partner can be found through personal contact, but in some cases this is not possible and an advertisement is placed in a reputable newspaper such as the *Times of India*.

Q: At what age do most arranged marriages take place?

Mr Sharma: It is usual now for the families to wait until their sons and daughters have completed their formal education before encouraging them to get married.

Of course, nowadays not every young Hindu accepts the idea of an arranged marriage, and many choose to find their own partner. Below are some ancient words of advice to parents seeking partners for their son or daughter:

'One should first examine the family of both the bride and bridegroom, those on the mother's side and on the father's side . . . One should give his daughter in marriage to a young man endowed with intelligence. One should marry a girl who possesses the characteristics of intelligence, beauty and good character and who is free from disease.'
(Asvalayana Grihya Sutra 1.5)

The Times of India
MATRIMONIALS FOR BRIDES

A Bombay Based North Indian Kshatriya (Goldsmith) youth 28 years, height 5'-6" from well settled respectable family having own business. Invites suitable alliance from respectable family. Preference for beautiful, sober and home loving educated girl. Advertisement for wider choice. Write xxx Times of India, Bombay 400 001.

A Mechanical Engineer Gujarzil Vaishnav Vanik 26 180 working in reputed company in Bombay drawing Rs. 3000-p.m. seeks marriage alliance from tall, vegetarian, well-educated, beautiful girls. Caste no bar. Advertisement for a wider choice. Parents may write to xxx Times of India, Bombay 400 001.

IAS/Allied Services Maharashtrian Brahmin boy 30/167 invites suitable alliance from respectable families. Preference for good looking, sober, and convent educated girl. Reply xxx Times of India, Bombay 400 001.

Looking For A Really Beautiful. tall, slim, fair, accomplished match for Punjabi Kshatriya status family, handsome, 180/26, B. Tech. (IIT Kanpur), MS. (USA). Green Card holder US $38 000, visiting India in May. Send details to xx Times of India, Bombay.

Educated, Good Looking Homely bride for 32/175, B.E. Hyderabad Kshatriya based army major – no bars. Apply xxx Times of India, Bombay 400 001.

Really Beautiful, Homely, Educated girl for very fair, handsome, smart, Bhopal settled Rajput businessman graduate, 35/170, own industry, monthly income high four figures, no caste bar, no dowry. Write xxx Times of India, New Delhi-2

BRIDE SLIM, AROUND 160–165, FOR HANDSOME, M.D., 27/172 BOY. DECENT PUNJABI ARORA FAMILY. IMMEDIATE MARRIAGE. CONTACT: WITHIN 4 DAYS. PHONE

Match for smart, well established, Industrialist Punjabi Khatri, having very good income, intelligent, Ahmedabad based, 25/178, Manglik, Vegetarian, Teetotaller, seeks hand of educated, pretty, homely girl of respectable family, aged 19/20. Write in Details to xxx Times of India, New Delhi-2.

Wanted Slim, Beautiful, Fair Complexioned well educated, preferably in English medium girl (below 25) for Bhumihar nationalised bank officer working around Delhi. Caste no bar. Lecturers/ bank officers preferable. Reply xx Times of India, New Delhi-2.

Telugu Girl For Vysya Community for youth, employed in Delhi, drawing handsome salary. Write xx Times of India, New Delhi-2.

Beautiful, Employed Girl For Scheduled caste handsome boy 27/172/1600/ B.Com., Delhi settled, govt. job, no bars, early marriage. Write xxx Times of India, New Delhi-2.

A Poona Based Tamilian Hindu boy 32/164 M.Sc. Class Two Officer seeks alliance from educated Tamil or Marathi speaking girls. Caste province status no bar. No dowry early simple marriage. View matrimony. Apply xxx Times of India, Bombay 400 001.

MATRIMONIALS FOR GROOMS

Manglik Non-Manglik Match for Brahmin girl, 28/164/2000, executive engineer/executive preferred. Caste no bar. Write xxx Times of India, New Delhi-2.

Army Officer, Doctor, Engineer, Garwali Brahmin match for smart, slim, homely B.Sc. Garwali Brahmin girl 160/22. Write xxx Times of India, New Delhi-2.

Wanted Officer Well Settled Preferably from Delhi for beautiful. Rajput, nursing officer in Army 25/158/1600. Caste no bar. Write xxx Times of India, New Delhi-2.

Proposals Invited From Post Graduate doctors of Nair community, for good looking lady doctor, doing house post Bombay, 25/158 cms. Write with horoscope, family details to xxx Times of India, New Delhi-2.

Suitable Matches For Saraswat Brahmin Haryana govt. employed beautiful two sisters. 28/164, M.Sc. M.Prim. 25/160, M.A. B.Ped. No bars. Preference officers or Delhi Haryana based. Write xxx Times of India, New Delhi-2.

Bengali Suitable Match for Vaisya girl 23 years, 150 cm, B.A., fair complexion, caste no bar. Write xxx Times of India, New Delhi-2.

Wanted Suitable Match for Convent educated beautiful Bengali Brahmin girl 22/158, M.A. B.Ed. from respectable family settled in Lucknow. Early marriage. Write xxx Times of India, Lucknow-1.

Suitable Matches For Twin, Sports sober girls height 156 cms. studying B.A. final, from business industrialist respectable Punjabi family. Write xxx Times of India, New Delhi-2.

Wanted A Suitable Match For 21 years, a pretty, tall, postgraduate Brahmin girl of distinguished family from a higher status Brahmin family. Preferably a businessman or services of rank & file. Write xxx Times of India, New Delhi-2.

Delhi Based South Indian Brahmin match for double post-graduate, beautiful, employed Andhra Brahmin girl, thirty. Write xxx Times of India, New Delhi-2.

A Suitable Match for Brahmin Girl 30, MA, wheatish, well connected family India and abroad, decent early marriage. Write xxx Times of India. New Delhi-2.

MATCH FOR FAIR COMPLEXIONED, ARORA PUNJABI GIRL 23/150 CMS, M.A. BELONGING RESPECTABLE FAMILY REQUIRED WELL PLACED BOY IN PROFESSION / BUSINESS / SERVICE FROM RESPECTABLE FAMILY, CASTE NO BARS. WRITE XXX TIMES OF INDIA, NEW DELHI-2.

A Hindu wedding in north London. Part of the ceremony involves joining the bride and groom with thread

The wedding

The traditional name for a Hindu wedding is **Kaniadan**, meaning the gift of a daughter. The actual date for the wedding is determined astrologically. The Vedas provide an ancient model for the Hindu marriage ritual, but the ceremony today varies widely according to each community.

'The Manusmriti says almost nothing at all about ritual details of marriage solemnisation. It merely lays down that a particular ritual, the **Saptapadi**, when completed with the seventh step, signifies legal validity of the marriage . . . The rite of saptapadi appears to have a special position even in present-day India and also in British Hindu marriages, but the Sanskrit texts that deal with marriage solemnisation in great detail are by no means uniform.'

(W.Menski, *Hinduism in Great Britain*)

Saptapadi ritual

The seven steps of **saptapadi** consecrate the marriage. Until the seventh step, any gift given to the bride is hers to keep. She receives presents and jewellery at this time. During the first six steps, six promises are made by the groom to the bride. On the seventh step the bride makes her promise to the groom. Only then is the marriage considered to have been completed.

In Britain the solemnisation of the marriage in a British registrar's office does not make the marriage valid in the eyes of the Hindu spouses and their families. They will, therefore, make arrangements for a Hindu wedding as well, which could be held any time up to several months later. Meanwhile, the couple would continue to live in their respective homes, without consummating the marriage. Some Hindu temples in Britain have been given the status of 'registered building' which means that the Hindu couple can register their marriage there and the Hindu rituals may be performed on the same day.

Divorce

Divorce is not really approved of within the Hindu tradition, since it is contrary to the idea of marriage as a sacrament – a holy and eternal bond between two people. Many of the lower castes have allowed divorce for some time on such grounds as the adultery or infertility of the woman, but this is still only possible with the consent of the caste council (usually the elder men of the caste), who do their best to help the couple to resolve their differences. In the past, such divorced women were forbidden from remarrying except amongst the lowest castes. A civil divorce is now available according to modern Indian law.

Below is one case which may well lead to a divorce:

Broken Marriage and Brawl Test a Cohesive Caste

By STEVEN R. WEISMAN
Special to The New York Times

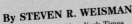

GURHA, India – After five years of marriage, Ganga walked out on her husband the other day, announcing that she would no longer submit to his beatings. She then returned to her parents in another part of this northern Indian village.

Village, caste and family have long been described as the building blocks of a society in which 75 percent of the population lives in rural areas. The recriminations surrounding the collapsed marriage of Ganga and her 22-year-old husband, Banwari, both from the low-caste group known as pasis, show what happens when all three come into collision.

The episode also reflects the practice among lower castes to resolve conflicts by holding mass meetings within their group. The tradition of such meetings is often cited by experts as demonstrating that India's democratic underpinnings are old and deep.

Caste Consciousness Strong

Discrimination on the basis of caste has been outlawed for decades in India, but caste consciousness remains as powerful as ever in Gurha and perhaps most of the country's 560 000 villages.

Many old forms of caste discrimination may be gone, but prejudices remain. Members of individual castes still refuse to marry members of other castes, and upper castes avoid many types of contact with lower ones . . . .

Mass Meeting Is Held

A few days after Ganga left for her parents, it was decided to hold a mass meeting of the pasi community to determine whether the marriage could be saved.

Witnesses said more than 500 people, a sizable part of the village, showed up to hear the couple and their relatives tell their stories under questioning from respected elders in the caste.

First, Banwari complained that his wife often left the house for long stretches, raising questions about her fidelity. But the meeting was said to have turned into an uproar when Ganga responded by accusing Banwari's father and uncle of trying to assault her sexually.

"It's impossible," the husband's father, Mata Prasad, said he replied. "Look at me. You can see that with my gray hair and at my age, I wouldn't do it."

He added that he might have gone to his son's house, reclined on a cot and sung songs – only out of joy for their marriage.

According to people who attended the meeting, most villagers felt that Ganga's and Banwari's marriage could be saved if the beatings stopped, and it was decreed that the couple should try to get back together.

(THE NEW YORK TIMES, Sunday, February 21, 1988)

Sati (Suttee)

According to the Hindu scriptures, a woman is only permitted to have one husband and is not allowed to remarry if her husband dies. This practice has been changed by Indian law, which permits the remarriage of widows and divorcees.

In some castes in Rajasthan there was an ancient practice called Sati, which still occurs there (though rarely) today.

'According to this practice, if a husband died (particularly at an early age), his wife would be permitted, encouraged and sometimes even forced to face death by burning herself along with the body of her husband on his funeral pyre.

Although the scriptures do not prescribe this practice, they do encourage it by considering this to be a good and noble act of deep devotion on the part of the widow, to give up her life when her husband is dead. Yet in the past it was rarely practised except in cases of defeat in battle, to prevent young wives falling into the hands of the enemy. Early in the nineteenth century the British rulers made the performance of sati illegal and this ban has continued. Yet occasionally a tragic case comes to light from a very remote and backward village community in which a woman is reported to have performed the rite of sati.'

(Damodar Sharma)

Such a case is reported here (*The Times*, 21 September 1987).

Mrs Kanwar at 18 is 'an example to womanhood'.

The way of a 'true wife'

Thousands flock to village site of suttee sacrifice

From Our Own Correspondent, Delhi

Of all the signs of how women are regarded in Indian society, perhaps the clearest is the reverence given to the suttee – the 'true wife' – who cradles her husband's head on her lap as his funeral pyre is lit and thus joins him in death.

Mrs Roop Kanwar, aged 18 when she died, is the latest in the steady flow of such suicides who are given the status of goddesses, have temples built to them, and are held up as shining examples of virtuous womanhood.

Mrs Kanwar was not an illiterate peasant but had been to secondary school. She had been married for eight months when her husband died and, reports say, she died willingly.

The site of her sacrifice, in Deorala village in Rajasthan, is now a place of pilgrimage. Eight or 10 young men with raised swords circle the spot unceasingly. Thousands of visitors, anxious to pay their respects, wear nylon rosettes to signify their intentions, and local merchants have given money for water kiosks to refresh them.

At least 200 000 people came to watch the last ceremony of the suttee last week, when a bridal sari was burned in the flames which had been fed by the sacrifices of devotees for the 12 days since it was originally lit. The fire was then put out with milk.

Although the state Government had banned the ceremonies and stopped all traffic to the village seven miles away, no one was deterred.

Mr Arvind Kala, a reporter for *The Statesman* newspaper, asked a few villagers: 'If it is all right for a woman to commit suttee, should not a man similarly immolate himself when his wife dies?'

One man gave him an answer which perfectly sums up society's view: 'Men should commit suttee also, but they don't have the strength. They aren't committed to their wives as the wives are to their husbands. But women? They are emotional. Their hearts rule their lives. They are capable of any sacrifice.'

Women's groups in the cities have long protested this attitude, which glorifies the lifelong sacrifice of a woman's identity as much as her physical sacrifice on the funeral pyre. They say an individual decision to commit suttee can scarcely be made.

As a writer in the *Hindustan Times* pointed out: 'Rural Indian society has scant regard for the individual. The clan, the village, the community, the caste group, the family – all have precedence over the individual. Decisions are made collectively by the leaders of these groups. In this environment the individual's ability to make an independent decision is severely limited.

'Can a rural woman who has no right to make the simplest decisions, who cannot step out of the home without the sanction of her family, make an independent decision to take her own life?'

Two researchers from Delhi University, who have made a study of some recent suttees, have pointed out that in those cases the villages in question were not isolated, but had close connections with nearby towns. The presumption then is that the suttees are a symptom of a desperate attempt by rural society to hold on to traditional feudal values in the face of increasing penetration by Western ideas of male/female equality.

The practice of suttee was abolished in 1829 by the enlightened Governor-General, Lord William Bentinck, and the Indian penal code today provides punishment for attempted suicide or abetting a suicide.

The Government, under pressure from educated opinion, has finally done something to show disapproval of the jamboree which is surrounding Mrs Kanwar's deification. The two senior officials responsible for law and order in the district have been posted elsewhere, and at the weekend her father-in-law and brother-in-law were charged with murder and abetting a suicide.

SEXUALITY

The sexuality of both humans and gods is spoken of quite freely in the shastras, although most Hindus are now reluctant to discuss this topic in public. Sexual intercourse is seen as reproducing the regenerative energy of the world. This notion is found in the representation in the Puranas of Shiva – the cosmic destroyer and regenerator – as the phallic symbol or **lingam**, which is lodged in the **yoni**, the female organ. (Many Hindus, however, regard the lingam as an abstract, philosophical symbol of diving creativity or of divine formlessness, and emphasize the importance of being able to see god in 'nothing'.) The act of making love is said to represent a sacred universal act of regeneration. This is clearly shown in the following verse from one of the Upanishads:

A Shivalingam

'Woman is a fire . . . the phallus is her fuel . . . when a man penetrates her, that is her coal; the ecstasy is her sparks. In this very fire, the gods offer semen; from this oblation, man comes to be. He lives out his allotted span. And when he dies, he is carried off to the funeral pyre. His fire becomes real fire.' (*Brihadaranyaka Upanishad* VI:2.13.)

Sensual pleasure, **kama**, is one of the acceptable areas of life that a Hindu can develop. Indeed, it is thought important that each person should understand his or her dependence on the senses in order to be able to control them, rather than be controlled by them. There is a strong emphasis on the need for self-control.

Children

'The woman nourishes the self of man which has entered into her. The woman carries him as an embryo.'
(Aitareya Upanishad 4.2,3.)

'Sons and daughters come from the same womb.'

Krishna and his brother as children, with the cowherds who looked after them

As we have seen, motherhood is a respected stage in a woman's life. The time of pregnancy is made much of in a Hindu family. It used to be the custom that a woman would go back to her mother's house two to three months before the birth of her child. She would then have the baby in a familiar environment and be cared for by her mother during what can be a very traumatic time. For about forty days after birth, she would be waited on by her mother, sisters and aunts and was not allowed into the kitchen to cook. (This is also because she is regarded as being ritually impure for ten days following the birth and in need of rest for at least another month.) Perhaps because of this family support, it is less common for Hindu women to suffer from post-natal depression.

Hindus feel that the attitude and behaviour of the parents influences the development of the new child's personality. Mahatma Gandhi writes:

'Children inherit the qualities of the parents, no less than their physical features. Environment does play an important part, but the original capital on which a child starts in life is inherited from its ancestors. I have also seen children successfully surmounting the effect of an evil inheritance. That is due to purity being an inherent attribute of the soul.'
(Autobiography)

Children in a north London school

BIRTH CONTROL

For the Hindu in India, as for Indians in general, children are regarded as a source of security in old age – someone to look after parents when they become old or ill. This is part of each Hindu child's duty. In the last century, it was thought important to have as many children as possible, in case they should die before the parents. The infant mortality rate was very high; sometimes only two or three children might survive out of a family of twelve. The introduction of antibiotics and better pre-and post-natal care means that now many more children survive to become adults. This has led to a tremendous population growth and has increased the poverty of the country.

The Indian Government has attempted to introduce a voluntary sterilisation programme in order to reduce the population increase and to lessen the burden of poverty. Vasectomy has been available to men for a long time and laproscopy has now been introduced for women. This involves a clamping of the fallopian tubes and is irreversible. Most of the younger generation will accept these forms of contraception, unless they have had no sons, but some of the older generation resent this attitude, desiring as many grandchildren as possible, and believing that sex is for procreation, not pleasure.

There are no specific prohibitions in Hinduism against the use of any form of contraceptive, although the most commonly used are those prescribed for women. Women are now taught about birth control in most ante-natal clinics in India, although until recently the topics of sex education and family planning were not discussed in most homes. With the introduction of education for girls as well as boys, it is possible for Hindu women to visit a female doctor in their neighbourhood. The doctor will have had a special training in gynaecology and obstetrics.

Abortion is considered to be immoral according to Hindu law, although is permitted in India. One group of western adherents of Hinduism have produced the following film critique dealing with the issue of abortion.

THE SILENT SCREAM
(Vaisnava Video)

For ten years, Dr. Bernard Nathanson was probably the most important abortion doctor in America. He certainly ran the biggest abortion clinic. Between 1968 and 1978 he presided over some 100 000 abortions. He personally carried out 5000 – at every stage of pregnancy.

But today, Bernard Nathanson is working on the other side – campaigning vigorously against abortion. Why? 'The science and technology of today,' says Dr. Nathanson, 'is revealing, at such a swift rate, the developments in the womb, that I gradually became convinced that what we have here is a human being. In the light of our knowledge today, no serious person could any longer talk about a "blob of jelly" in the way that we used to.'

Dr. Nathanson has made a film which, he believes, will show the world more acutely than ever before the actuality of abortion practice. Entitled The Silent Scream, it is a visual recording of what happens inside the woman's womb during the abortion of an 11-week foetus – not considered a very late stage of development.

Using the techniques of ultrasound film, Dr. Nathanson photographed the operation from within the womb. 'The results,' he says, 'show the unborn infant recoil from the abortion instrument, thrash about in excruciating agony, open its mouth and emit a silent scream as it is attacked and destroyed.' The film provoked a storm of distressed protest when a rough cut was shown on Australian television – thousands of people had seen, for the first time, what actually happens when an unborn child is removed from the womb. 'Obviously the pro-abortionists don't like my film', comments Dr. Nathanson, 'so I say – "okay, go make one of your own". But it doesn't matter who makes it. The evidence is the evidence. The camera would see the same thing each time.'

The Silent Scream is a disturbing film – but just one more visual testimony to the pressing need our modern society has for change.   (ISKON)

Activities

1. (a) With your neighbour discuss what the concept 'family' means to you (e.g. who are the members of a family, what relationships does the term cover?).

   (b) It is sometimes said that a stable family structure can lead to a stable society, which in turn leads to a more peaceful world. Do you think this is true? Write down your ideas, with explanations.

   (c) Think about the main causes of both the collapse and continuation of the family structure in British society. List these in two columns. Now do the same, from a Hindu perspective. Are there any similarities or differences in your lists?

2. (a) From your reading of the introductory section and the chapter on Work and wealth, summarise the main family duties and personal duties of both a Hindu man and woman. This may be done in the form of a radio or television interview.

   (b) From the page of quotations about the role of women, choose two contrasting passages or sentences. Use them to begin two separate diary entries, imagining that you were the woman being spoken about.

3. Now read the section on Choosing a partner very carefully.

   (a) With your neighbour, discuss the 'fors' and 'againsts' of having a partner chosen for you by your family. Make two lists of these.

   (b) What criteria would you look for if choosing a suitable partner for your child (e.g. wealth, family background)? Write out a newspaper advertisement for a suitable partner. In what ways does your advertisement differ from those examples from the *Times of India*?

   (c) Cut out some adverts for partners from the 'Personal' column of a newspaper or magazine and compare these also. List the main differences and similarities.

4. Mahatma Gandhi was not unhappily married, despite the early age of this commitment.

   (a) What arguments can *you* find against 'preposterously early marriages'? Write these down.

   (b) What do you consider to be the appropriate age, or time in life, for someone to get married? Give reasons for your answer.

   (c) Look up the word **sacrament**. Explain how the Hindu marriage is regarded as a sacrament. Does this view coincide with your own ideas about marriage? Explain clearly why/why not.

5. (a) Make a list of the people who have influenced your life so far, in order of importance (e.g. parents, teachers, sports players). Now write down the ways in which those people have influenced you.

   (b) Do you agree with Gandhi that people 'inherit the qualities of their parents', or does environment play a significant part as well?

   (c) In what ways does the Hindu belief that 'purity is an attribute of the soul' affect the way they regard unborn children in the womb and children in their first few years of life?

Research

Find out more about the laws regarding marriage and divorce in Britain.

1. Conduct a survey in class to discover what most people your age feel about the commitment of marriage. Make up four or five relevant questions. You might like to compare the response to that of people from other age groups.

2. Hold a debate in class, with an 'open floor', on the topic 'Religious Law is more important to the individual than Civil Law'.

Dictionary words

KAMA	SATI
KANIADAN	LINGAM
SAPTAPADI	YONI

DRUGS • DRUGS • DRUGS • DRUGS • DRUGS • DRUGS • DRUGS • DRUGS • DRUGS • DRUGS • DRUGS • DRUGS • DRUGS • DRUGS • DRUGS • DR

Drugs

UGS • DRUGS • DRUGS • DRUGS • DRUGS • DRUGS • DRUGS • DRUGS • DRUGS • DRUGS • DRUGS • DRUGS • DRUGS • DRUGS • DRUGS • DR

DRUG DEPENDENCY

The Indian government, in agreement with international drug treaties, now legislates heavily against the illegal use and sale of non-prescribed drugs. Formerly the government attitude towards drug-taking was more relaxed, although moderation was always advocated.

There is no scriptural prohibition against drug-taking within the Hindu scriptures. Indeed, the Vedas mention the use of a powerful substance, **Soma**, as being essential to the rituals. It is not known exactly what Soma was. But many Hindus now have strong reservations about the consumption of any intoxicating drink.

Soma

Soma was primarily the offering made to the god Indra, but seems to have been used in sacrifices to all the gods. It was probably drunk by both the priests and the worshippers during certain rituals. Some scholars say it was the hallucinogenic mushroom, *Amanita Muscaria*, and others that it was an alcoholic or hallucinogenic beverage caused by fermenting a certain plant. In the *Rig Veda*, Soma is said to make men courageous, to cure illness and to bring immortality, prosperity and brave sons. It was obviously not regarded as a harmful drug when taken as part of the religious ritual. Here are some verses from the *Rig Veda* about the power of Soma.

This hymn celebrates the effects of Soma, particularly the feeling of being set free and released into boundless open space, and the belief that the drinker is immortal.

We Have Drunk the Soma

I have tasted the sweet drink of life, knowing that it inspires good thoughts and joyous expansiveness to the extreme, that all the gods and mortals seek it together, calling it honey.

We have drunk the Soma; we have become immortal; we have gone to the light; we have found the gods. What can hatred and the malice of a mortal do to us now, O immortal one?

When we have drunk you, O drop of Soma, be good to our heart, kind as a father to his son, thoughtful as a friend to a friend. Far-famed Soma, stretch out our life-span so that we may live.

The glorious drops that I have drunk set me free in wide space. You have bound me together in my limbs as thongs bind a chariot. Let the drops protect me from the foot that stumbles and keep lameness away from me.

Inflame me like a fire kindled by friction; make us see far; make us richer, better. For when I am intoxicated with you, Soma, I think myself rich. Draw near and make us thrive.

We would enjoy you, pressed with a fervent heart, like riches from a father. King Soma, stretch out our life-spans as the sun stretches the spring days.

Weaknesses and diseases have gone; the forces of darkness have fled in terror. Soma has climbed up in us, expanding. We have come to the place where they stretch out life-spans.

(*Rig Veda* 8:48. 1, 3–7, 11)

35

The Soma-Drinker Praises Himself

This, yes, this is my thought: I will win a cow and
a horse. Have I not drunk Soma?

Like impetuous winds, the drinks have lifted me
up. Have I not drunk Soma?

The drinks have lifted me up, like swift horses
bolting with a chariot. Have I not drunk Soma?

The prayer has come to me as a lowing cow
comes to her beloved son. Have I not drunk
Soma?

I turn the prayer around in my heart, as a wheel-
wright turns a chariot seat. Have I not drunk
Soma?

(*Rig Veda*, 10.119.1–5
translated by W. O'Flaherty)

Alcohol

Most Hindus would refer to the use of Soma in the Veda as evidence that the consumption of alcohol is permitted, although alcohol is never offered at public functions and is considered by many to be a social evil. It would, for example, be a cause of great offence even for non-Hindus to visit a temple in the afternoon after consuming alcohol at lunch-time.

According to the Indian constitution, the prohibition of alcohol is a 'directive principle', that is, it is a directive from the government which is strongly recommended, but is left to the discretion of each state to administer. In Gujarat, a province of India, alcohol is totally prohibited. Other states have partial prohibition, restricting the days or times of drinking. There are very few 'drinking houses' in India and those which do exist tend to sell locally made alcohol and to be patronised by the lower castes.

One modern Hindu poet, Hari Vansha Rai, has, however, written some light-hearted lines about the hypocrisy of those people who do not drink alcohol on moral grounds, but who also show no love or compassion for those less fortunate than themselves. He is perhaps trying to make the point that just as God is not limited to one 'holy' place, so a human's moral awareness should extend to all areas of life.

'O God, you are a cheater,
We thought you lived in a temple.
But you live in a drinking-house.'

(Hari Vansha Rai)

International control of drugs

The world-wide control of narcotic drugs and psychotropic substances has been developed gradually over the last 70 years by a number of international treaties which finally resulted in the adoption of the Single Convention on Narcotic Drugs in 1961. This was amended by the 1972 Protocol and in the Convention on Psychotropic Substances of 1971 . . . .

Two categories of drugs are controlled by the international drug treaties, namely narcotic drugs and psychotropic substances. At present, control is exercised over 105 narcotic drugs and some 80 psychotropic substances. The narcotic drugs include opium and its derivatives, morphines, codeine and heroin, other synthetic narcotics such as methadone and pethidine, and cannabis and cocaine. These drugs are controlled under the provisions of the 1961 Single Convention and of the 1972 Protocol. – The International Narcotics Control Board (INCB)

The overall task of the INCB is to promote compliance by governments with the various drug control treaties in the interest of the international community as a whole. It has to administer the legal movement of narcotic drugs and psychotropic substances with the precise aim of limiting their production, manufacture, trade and use exclusively to medical and scientific needs. In cooperation with governments, it ensures that legitimate demand for narcotic drugs is satisfied through the maintenance of a proper balance between supply and demand. And it tries to prevent the illegal or illicit cultivation, production, manufacture, traffic and use of drugs.

(B. Juppin de Fondaumière)

Smoking in the Third World by Uma Ram Nath

The cycle of tobacco use, disease, debate and public action that is already familiar in developed countries of the world is only just starting up in the Third World.

The fact is that drugs – all kinds of drugs – constitute very big business throughout the world. In Zimbabwe, tobacco production is the nation's largest industry. In Malawi, 100 000 families rely on cash from tobacco, while in the Indian state of Andhra Pradesh, tobacco provides a living for 75 000 farmers and about two million other workers are engaged in curing, packing and processing . . .

In India, total cigarette consumption rose 400 per cent between 1970 and 1980 . . .

While cigarette manufacturers are endeavouring to sell the low tar cigarette in an attempt to make their product appear 'safe' to 'Western' consumers, their products bearing international brand names, but sold in the developing world, have much higher yields of tar and nicotine . . . Cigarettes sold in China, India and Pakistan have a high tar and nicotine content . . .

In India, changes to the excise tax structure resulted in the flooding of the market by new and competing brands. As the more expensive cigarettes fell within a higher tax bracket, their sales dropped. Challengers to the main producers are now offering cheaper cigarettes and in a plethora of brands. And the Indian smoker has taken these up.

(Article taken from 'World Health', June 1986)

Tobacco

Tobacco is used in several different forms in India, none of which is considered to be particularly harmful unless one becomes addicted to them. For instance, some old men and women take 'naska', a tobacco powder which is sniffed up the nose rather like snuff. Tobacco paste is often added to the popular 'pan' (see below) and smoking is quite permissible, although its harmful effects on an unborn child and on the lungs of the smoker are recognised. Many villagers still chew tobacco leaves and some smoke 'bidis', the traditional Indian cigarette, with the tobacco rolled in a tobacco leaf instead of cigarette paper.

Mahatma Gandhi wrote about the attitude towards smoking during his childhood in India in the late nineteenth century. In an account from his autobiography he tells of the trouble that smoking got him into:

'A relative and I became fond of smoking. Not that we saw any good in smoking, or were enamoured of the smell of a cigarette. We simply imagined a sort of pleasure in emitting clouds of smoke from our mouths. My uncle had the habit and when we saw him smoking, we thought we should copy his example. But we had no money. So we began pilfering stumps of cigarettes thrown away by my uncle.

The stumps, however, were not always available, and could not emit much smoke, either. So we began to steal copper coins from the servant's pocket money in order to purchase Indian cigarettes. But the question was where to keep them. We could not of course smoke in the presence of elders. We managed somehow for a few weeks on these stolen coppers. In the meantime we heard that the stalks of certain plants were porous and could be smoked like cigarettes. We got them and began this kind of smoking . . .

Ever since I have grown up, I have never desired to smoke and have always regarded the habit of smoking as barbarous, dirty and harmful. I have never understood why there is such a rage for smoking throughout the world. I cannot bear to travel in a compartment full of people smoking. I become choked.'

(Autobiography)

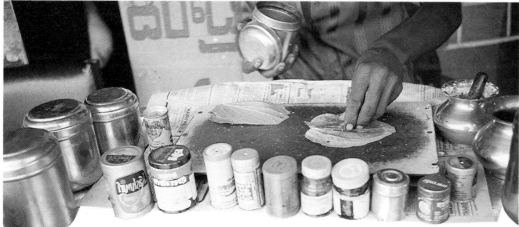
Pan being made

Pan

Pan is a popular 'snack', taken by both men and women. It is the Indian equivalent of chewing gum. It consists of rose leaves, betel nut, red paste and 'chuna' (lime), all wrapped up in a betel leaf. It is said not to be addictive, although it does have a stimulating and narcotic effect. The whole pan is eaten as a digestive and swallowed, unless tobacco paste is added; in this case, the mixture is very strong and the pan is just chewed for a while before being spat out.

Coffee and tea

Coffee and tea are both stimulants. Tea, like coffee, is not indigenous to India, but was introduced centuries ago from China, and has been a favourite beverage there for several generations. Although both coffee and tea are socially acceptable drinks, they do contain addictive substances. This is what one Hindu thinker said about habitual coffee drinkers:

'Some feel the need of coffee in the morning, and without it they get a headache. The body may not have required it at first, but it has gradually got used to the pleasurable taste and stimulation of coffee, and now it suffers when deprived of it . . . The habit is formed when there is pleasure and the demand for the continuation of the pleasure. Habit is based on pleasure and the memory of it . . . To be inwardly alert, to think anew about your work, about the absurdities of society, to find out for yourself the true significance of religion – it is this that will free the mind from being enslaved by any habit.'

(J. Krishnamurti)

Women workers on a tea plantation, India

Addiction

According to traditional Hindu teaching, the inward craving which is a characteristic of drug addiction causes such negative states as mental confusion, fear, depression, sleepiness, wretchedness, anger and lack of rational and emotional balance. This is obviously not a healthy state to be in. In fact these qualities are said to belong to the darker side of human nature. Most drugs are therefore regarded as being unhealthy in that they do not promote a fuller life, strength or energy, but induce only a temporary sense of pleasure and well-being.

Cannabis or Marihuana

The products of the plant *Cannabis sativa* have been used by millions of people as an intoxicant over the last four or five thousand years. It is used in various forms. People smoke it, often combined with tobacco, or mix its resin with drinks or in sweetmeats. Such use is still tolerated in certain countries.

Cannabis has become, from the medical point of view, an obsolete remedy. It has therefore been recommended that its use be discontinued in medical practice, but it is still used for the treatment of certain ailments by local medical practitioners in some countries in Asia.

In certain countries, the consumption of cannabis has been a traditional custom for centuries, particularly in those regions where the consumption of alcohol is prohibited.

(Single Convention on Narcotic Drugs, 1961)

Marihuana (Cannabis)

'Cannabis plant' means any plant of the genus *cannabis*. 'Cannabis resin' means the separate resin, whether crude or purified, obtained from the cannabis plant

Marihuana was discovered 5000 years ago. The plant, Cannabis sativa, grows in mild climates throughout the world especially Mexico, Africa, India and the Middle East. The strength of the drug differs from place to place, depending on where and how it is grown, how it is prepared and how it is stored.

Traffickers frequently include all parts of the plant including seeds and stalks – sometimes grass, alfalfa, other drugs or diluents – in marihuana preparations. Sophisticated abusers insist on and pay high premiums for the more potent preparations of cannabis resin or the female flowering top of the plant. In 1966, a scientist synthesized the active ingredient of marihuana, tetrahydro-cannabinol. (THC).

Abusers usually smoke marihuana in cigarettes, hookahs or pipes with small bowls. Some smokers make removable tin foil bowls to hold the marihuana. They also use wire 'roach holders' or paper clips to smoke the whole cigarette.

Although there is now heavy legislation against the misuse of cannabis in India, in the past it was regarded as not particularly harmful, and even useful if taken in moderation. Its use in the past may be compared with the British approach to the taking of laudanum and other forms of morphine in the nineteenth century.

In the *Shivapurana*, Lord Shiva is spoken of as the patron of cannabis. The use of cannabis is referred to in that text. Until the present laws, it was fairly commonly used. Middle-aged Indians now recall putting crumbled cannabis into pakoras to eat during the festival of Holi. Although it is still used by some Indian sects to aid meditation and the reaching of a 'higher state of consciousness', the shastras condemn this, claiming that drugs benumb the senses and mind. In meditation, the mind must be active and not numb.

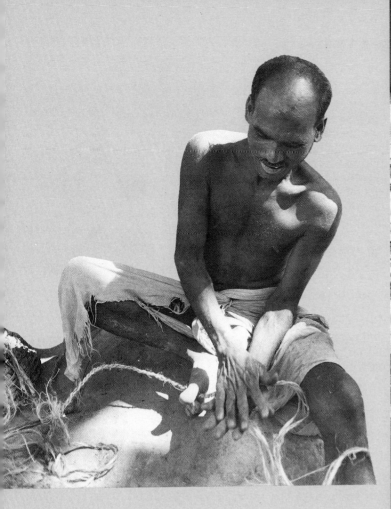

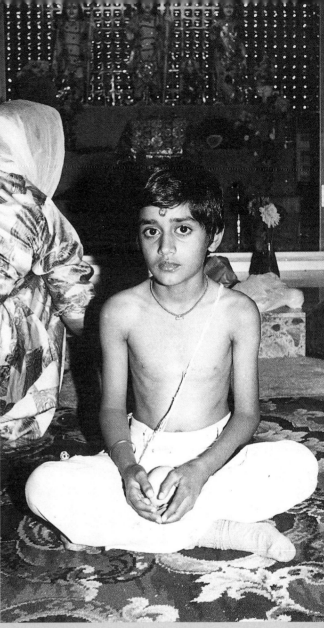

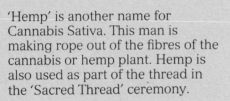

'Hemp' is another name for Cannabis Sativa. This man is making rope out of the fibres of the cannabis or hemp plant. Hemp is also used as part of the thread in the 'Sacred Thread' ceremony.

Opium

The products of the opium poppy were more commonly used in India forty or fifty years ago than now, largely due to government legislation. Just as some people now take prescribed sleeping tablets, which contain an opium derivative or chemical equivalent, so Indian mothers used to help their children to sleep with a small dose of opium. Nowadays, opium is recognised as a vital basis for many medicines. This stems from its use as a sedative and pain-reliever throughout the East Asian countries.

From the Puranic references, opium was apparently given to soldiers in order to stop them from being afraid and to give them the courage to fight. It numbed the pain if they were wounded. It is said to cause constipation – a useful asset if on the march or in the middle of battle!

In the days of the regional rulers or maharajas early this century, opium was taken in court on special occasions such as the ruler's birthday or the festival of Dusshera. In Rajasthan, a province in North-West India, it was considered an honour to receive the liquid opiate from the cupped palm of the maharajas.

NATURAL AND SYNTHETIC OPIATES

The earliest recorded knowledge of opium is to be found in the Sumerian tablets. Sumerians lived in Lower Mesopotamia (modern Iraq) around 5000 BCE. Later, knowledge of the poppy's medicinal properties was introduced to Persia and Egypt by the Babylonians. The Greeks and Arabs also used opium for medicinal purposes. The first recorded instance of poppy cultivation in India dates from the eleventh century, and production and consumption of opium in that country became extensive in the sixteenth century during Mongol rule.

Morphine

Morphine is the main active principle of opium. The average morphine content of opium is about 10 per cent. Morphine is extracted either from opium or, directly, from the poppy straw (the dried capsules and the upper part of the stems of the opium poppy after mowing). The use of the poppy straw process eliminates the production of opium and greatly reduces all risks of abuse and illicit traffic. This process has expanded greatly and, in recent years, about one third of the world's medical requirements for morphine has been manufactured from poppy straw.

Opium poppy

'Opium poppy' means the plant of the species *Papaver somniferum L.* 'Opium' means the coagulated juice of the opium poppy

Drugs obtained from the opium poppy: morphine and heroin

Doctors prescribe morphine to relieve pain, but addicts rank it second to heroin. They may abuse morphine when heroin is scarce.

Codeine is most frequently abused when in cough syrups, but occasionally the pure drug is abused. Its effects are milder when compared to heroin and morphine.

(Single Convention on Narcotic Drugs, 1961)

Morphine was widely used for the relief of short-term acute pain resulting from surgery, fractures and burns and in the final stages of terminal illnesses. Through the introduction of synthetic narcotics and other analgesic drugs, the extent of use and the therapeutic importance of morphine have been considerably diminished (but it is still considered to be the prototype of the narcotic drug).

Codeine and other morphine derivatives

Codeine, an effective cough suppressant, is one of the most commonly and widely employed medicaments. Codeine (methylmorphine) occurs in opium in low concentration, but for the market is manufactured principally by the conversion of morphine. This explains the apparent contradiction between the decrease in the therapeutic use of morphine and the increase in its production: more than 90 per cent of the morphine produced by the pharmaceutical industry is converted into codeine. It has properties which resemble those of morphine but its analgesic effects are milder.

Cases of codeine addiction are relatively rare, as dependence develops only after continued consumption of large quantities over a considerable period of time.

Heroin

Heroin (diacetylmorphine) is derived from morphine.

('World Health', June 1986)

> Now developed and developing countries alike are struggling to contain what has been termed 'the global heroin economy,' which includes street dealing in Manhattan, the problems of opium farmers in India, Pakistan, Sri Lanka and Thailand, and smuggling networks which criss-cross the world's airways and oceans. Heroin use is spreading in poppy-growing countries themselves.
>
> ('World Health', June 1986)

DRUGS AS MEDICINE

Perhaps one of the most controversial issues connected with drug-taking concerns the possibility of a person becoming addicted to a drug which is taken because of an illness. A question which arises is whether it is preferable to suffer the pain of what may be a terminal illness, such as cancer, or to face the thought of needing to depend upon a chemical substance, taken in ever-increasing quantities for the rest of one's life.

Here is one Hindu philosopher's answer. Others think very differently, although many choose to use a combination of 'Western' and 'Eastern' medicines in trying to cure themselves.

'Though I have had two serious illnesses in my life, I believe that man has little need to drug himself. 999 cases out of a thousand can be brought round by means of a well-regulated diet, water and earth treatment and similar household remedies. He who runs to the doctor for every little ailment, and swallows all kinds of vegetable and mineral drugs, not only curtails his life, but by becoming the slave of his body instead of remaining its master, loses self-control and ceases to be a person.'

(J. Krishnamurti)

Activities

1.

> 'Most people have this feeling of loneliness, this sense of isolation, with its fear, only they smother it, run away from it, get themselves lost in some form of activity . . . . In their fear of being lonely, of feeling cut off, some take to drink, others take drugs, while many turn to politics or find some other way of escape.'
>
> (J. Krishnamurti)

(a) With your neighbour, discuss other reasons why people may turn to alcohol or drug-taking. Make a list of these reasons.

(b) What might Krishnamurti have suggested might be the best approach to loneliness?

(c) In your opinion, is experimentation with drugs:
  i) an abuse of the body;
  ii) a necessary branch of medical research;
  iii) a valid attempt to experience an alternative view of the world?

Discuss this in class, then write down your thoughts in the form of a newspaper article.

(d) Imagine that you are a doctor. Using some of the ideas in this section, what advice might you give concerning pain relief to a patient suffering from an illness?

2.

> 'Any nation will drink more alcohol, smoke more cigarettes or abuse more opiates if the relevant drug is made more available. The key to reducing drug — and alcohol — related problems lies in controlling production, marketing, retailing and distribution.'
>
> (Anthony W. Clare)

(a) Do you agree with this statement?

(b) If so, how would you set about bringing in some form of control? If not, what other approaches could be taken to solve the problems?

3. (a) Do you think cigarette smoking should be banned altogether in all public places (e.g. restaurants, pubs, on public transport)? Make two columns and list the 'fors' and 'againsts'. Which has more reasons? Which reasons are stronger? Why?

(b) What do you think Mahatma Gandhi would have said to this question? Write down a possible response he might have given.

Research

a) Try to find out more about the current British legislation on the taking of drugs, particularly marijuana, opiates, alcohol and tobacco. You could write to agencies such as Alcoholics Anonymous, Release, or the Health Education Council for further information.

(b) Find out which religions do and do not condemn the consumption of drugs, alcohol and tobacco. What are their reasons for these prohibitions?

Dictionary words

HEMP	NARCOTIC
CANNABIS SATIVA	HALLUCINOGEN
ADDICTION	

Peace and Conflict

'To see the universal and all-pervading spirit of Truth face to face one must be able to love the meanest of creation as oneself.'
(Mahatma Gandhi)

Gandhi's statement is a basic summary of the traditional Hindu approach to peace: if one human being truly loves all other living beings, then cruelty and violence towards others are impossible. Gandhi claimed that peace does not prevail because people do not adopt this attitude of love. He said,

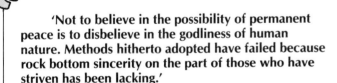

'Not to believe in the possibility of permanent peace is to disbelieve in the godliness of human nature. Methods hitherto adopted have failed because rock bottom sincerity on the part of those who have striven has been lacking.'

He also said,

'If recognised leaders of mankind who have control over the engines of destruction were wholly to renounce their use with full knowledge of the implications, permanent peace can be obtained.'

Gandhi's thoughts are echoed in these words by Krishnamurti,

'The world isn't made better through hate and envy. Aren't you seeking power and position rather than to bring about a world in which all hate, greed and violence have come to an end? . . . Hate can only breed further hate; and a society based on hate, on envy, a society in which there are competing groups, each safeguarding its own interests – such a society will always be at war within itself, and so with other societies . . . . Such a society may and generally does profess to believe in love, in goodness, but it is always ready to kill, to go to war.'

GANDHI'S VIEW OF NON-VIOLENCE (AHIMSA)

The concept of **Ahimsa**, usually translated as 'non-violence' or 'non-injury', is at least as old as the Vedas, which contain the words, 'Do not kill any living being'. For Gandhi, real love was shown when one could meet violence with non-violence. Gandhi applied the concept of ahimsa to daily life and gave it the widest possible meaning, identifying it as an aspect of truth or God. 'The individual can only realise the truth through a complete merging of oneself in, and identification with, this limitless ocean of life.' All people have the spark of non-violence or love in them; the best way, therefore, of overcoming evil is not to kill the evildoers, but to change their hearts by refusing to retaliate. The only way of overcoming hatred and cruelty of any kind is through passive resistance, motivated by love of all life.

'The moral to be legitimately drawn from the supreme tragedy of the bomb is that it will not be destroyed by counter bombs, even as violence cannot be destroyed by counter violence. Mankind has got to get out of violence only through non-violence. Hatred can be overcome only by love.' (*Harijan*, July 7, 1946)

For Gandhi, there are six 'prerequisites' which the believer in non-violence must adopt:
1.   It must be taken for granted that non-violence is the law meant for rational beings. It is therefore preferable to brute force, which is the law of the jungle.
2.   The believer in non-violence must have a living faith in God.
3.   Non-violence should be taken to be the best defence of a person's self-respect and should not be used as the means to protect personal property or wealth.
4.   Non-violence means self-sacrifice. This means that to possess other people's property and countries is immoral.
5.   The power of non-violence is available to all. It does not depend on caste, creed and age, only on one's faith in the God of love. It should therefore be accepted as the law of life.
6.   The law of love, non-violence, which is the law of life, can be applied to the local community as well as to the whole of humanity.

A practical demonstration of non-violent non-cooperation

Gandhi's own faith in the power of non-violence as a moral equivalent to war was shown during the mass movements of **Satyagraha** (non-violent protest) against the British government in India.

   The successful use of non-violence in a political situation was shown by the Satyagrahis (truth marchers) who defied the British government's ban on the Indian preparation of salt near Bombay in 1930. An American journalist, Webb Miller, reported the event in the following words:

'In complete silence Gandhi men drew up and halted a hundred yards from the stockade. A picked column advanced from the crowd, waded the ditches and approached the barbed wire stockade . . . Suddenly at a word of command, scores of native policemen rushed upon the advancing marchers and rained blows on their heads with their steel-shod lathis. Not one of the marchers even raised an arm to fend off the blows. They went down like ninepins. From where I stood I heard the sickening whack of the club on unprotected skulls. The waiting crowd of marchers groaned and sucked in their breath in sympathetic pain of every blow. Those struck down fell sprawling, unconscious or writhing with fractured skulls or broken shoulders . . . .The survivors, without breaking ranks, silently and doggedly marched on until struck down.'

'Although everyone knew that within a few minutes he would be beaten down, perhaps killed, I could detect no signs of wavering or fear. They marched steadily with hands up, without the encouragement of music or cheering or any possibility that they might escape serious injury or death. The police rushed out and mechanically beat down the second column. There was no fight, no struggle, the marchers simply walked forward till struck down.'
(*The Life of Mahatma Gandhi* L. Fischer)

A former Hindu Prime Minister of India, Jawahar Lal Nehru, adopted Gandhi's policy of non-violence and promoted it in the world of international politics. He banned the production of atomic bombs in India, although its scientists were capable of making them. He also laid down five ethical principles for the peaceful co-existence of the nations of the world. These are the Five Principles, the *Pancasila*:

---

(1) Respect for the territorial integrity and sovereignty of other nations.

(2) Non-aggression, i.e. avoiding armed attack on other nations.

(3) Non-interference in the domestic affairs of other nations.

(4) Maintaining equality and mutual benefit with regard to trade and commerce with other nations.

(5) Peaceful co-existence, i.e. toleration for the ideology of other nations.

Within a year of their formulation, these broad principles of conduct for all nations were adopted by more than thirty countries.

WAR AS A MEANS TO PEACE

The place of non-violence in the Indian tradition has been emphasised, but throughout India's history, the waging of war has been part of political life. The 'warrior caste', the *kshatriya*, were also the rulers.

In the *Rig Veda*, the early Aryans appear as a militaristic people, glorying in their ability to strike terror in their enemies. Their chief god, Indra, is a warrior. Here is how Indra is described in the *Rig Veda*:

'Who is Indra?'

The god who had insight the moment he was born, the first who protected the gods with his power of thought, before whose hot breath the two world-halves tremble at the greatness of his manly powers – he, my people, is Indra.

He who made fast the tottering earth, who made still the quaking mountains, who measured out and extended the expanse of the air, who propped up the sky – he, my people, is Indra.

He who killed the serpent and loosed the seven rivers, who drove out the cows that had been pent up by Vala, who gave birth to fire between two stones, the winner of booty in combats – he, my people, is Indra.

He by whom all these changes were rung, who drove the race of Dāsas down into obscurity, who took away the flourishing wealth of the enemy as a winning gambler takes the stake – he, my people, is Indra.

He about whom they ask, 'Where is he?', or they say of him, the terrible one, 'He does not exist', he who diminishes the flourishing wealth of the enemy as gambling does – believe in him! He, my people, is Indra.

He who encourages the weary and the sick, and the poor priest who is in need, who helps the man who harnesses the stones to press Soma, he who has lips fine for drinking – he, my people, is Indra.

He under whose command are horses and cows and villages and all chariots, who gave birth to the sun and the dawn and led out the waters, he, my people, is Indra.

He who is invoked by both of two armies, enemies locked in combat, on this side and that side, he who is even invoked separately by each of two men standing on the very same chariot, he, my people, is Indra.

He without whom people do not conquer, he whom they call on for help when they are fighting, who

(continued)

became the image of everything, who shakes the unshakeable – he, my people, is Indra.

He who killed with his weapon all those who had committed a great sin, even when they did not know it, he who does not pardon the arrogant man for his arrogance, who is the slayer of the Dasyus, he, my people, is Indra.

He who in the fortieth autumn discovered Sambara living in the mountains, who killed the violent serpent, the Dānu, as he lay there, he, my people, is Indra.

(Rig Veda, 2:12)

One hymn in the *Rig Veda* is a blessing of weapons before a battle. Each item is described separately and praised:

To Arms

With the bow let us win cows, with the bow let us win the contest and violent battles with the bow. The bow ruins the enemy's pleasure; with the bow let us conquer all the corners of the world.

She comes all the way up to your ear like a woman who wishes to say something, embracing her dear friend; humming like a woman, the bowstring stretched tight on the bow carries you safely across in the battle.

These two who go forward like a woman going to an encounter hold the arrow in their lap as a mother holds a son. Let the two bow-tips, working together, pierce our enemies and scatter our foes.

Standing in the chariot, the skilful charioteer drives his prize-winning horses forward wherever he wishes to go. Praise the power of the reins: the guides follow the mind that is behind them.

Neighing violently, the horses with their showering hoofs outstrip everyone with their chariots. Trampling down the foes with the tips of their hoofs, they destroy their enemies without veering away.

The wagon of transport – oblation is its name – on which the weapons and armour are placed, on it let us place the working chariot and be of good heart all our days.

(Rig Veda, 6:75)

For the author of the *Bhagavad Gita*, war was seen as a part of the caste-duty of the warrior/ruler. For a person who has not renounced the world, the task allotted to one's caste must be performed. Krishna, the charioteer, says to the Prince Arjuna who does not want to fight his cousins:

'Likewise consider thine own caste-duty
Then too hast thou no cause to tremble,
For nothing is better than a fight
Prescribed by duty for a man of the princely class.

Happy the warriors indeed
Who become involved in war
Like this, presented by pure chance
And opening the gates of paradise.

But if thou wilt not wage this war
Prescribed by thy duty,
Then by casting off both honour and duty
Thou wilt bring evil on thyself.

Yes, this dishonour will become a byword
In the mouths of men in ages yet to come.'

(Bhagavad Gita 2:31–34)

Krishna as charioteer

HIMSA

Even Mahatma Gandhi, despite his commitment to non-violence, acknowledged that,

'the very fact of living – eating, drinking and moving about – necessarily involves some *himsa*, destruction of life, be it ever so minute . . . So long as a person continues to be a social being, he cannot but participate in the *himsa* that the very existence of society involves. When two nations are fighting, the duty of an advocate of ahimsa is to stop the war. He who is not equal to that duty, he who has no power of resisting war, he who is not qualified to resist war, may take part in war, and yet wholeheartedly try to free himself, his nation and the world from war.'   (M.K. Gandhi, *Autobiography*)

Gandhi himself enlisted as a volunteer and did ambulance work in India in the First World War.

There seem, therefore, to be two different attitudes within the Hindu tradition towards the act of killing. These are presented in the two extracts below. Read them very carefully and consider whether they can be reconciled with each other.

(a)   There are many forms of killing, are there not? There is killing by a word or a gesture, killing in fear or in anger, killing for a country or an ideology, killing for a set of economic dogmas or religious beliefs.

'How does one kill by a word or a gesture?'

Don't you know? With a word or a gesture you may kill a man's reputation; through gossip, defamation, contempt, you may wipe him out. And does not comparison kill? Don't you kill a boy by comparing him with another who is cleverer or more skilful? A man who kills out of hate or anger is regarded as a criminal and put to death. Yet the man who deliberately bombs thousands of people off the face of the earth in the name of his country is honoured, decorated; he is looked upon as a hero. Killing is spreading over the earth. For the safety or expansion of one nation, another is destroyed. Animals are killed for food, for profit, or for so-called sport; they are vivisected for the 'well-being' of man. The soldier exists to kill. Extraordinary progress is being made in the technology of murdering vast numbers of people in a few seconds and at great distances. Many scientists are wholly occupied with it, and priests bless the bomber and the warship. Also, we kill a cabbage or a carrot in order to eat; we destroy a pest. Where are we to draw the line beyond which we will not kill?   (Krishnamurti)

(b)   This quotation is from the *Bhagavad Gita*. The 'embodied self' is the **atman** which is permanent and cannot therefore be killed. Since human life is temporary and everyone dies, Arjuna is told by Krishna not to try to preserve life, but rather to recognise that the atman is beyond birth and death.

Our bodies are known to end,
but the embodied self is enduring,
indestructible, and immeasurable;
therefore, Arjuna, fight the battle!

He who thinks this self a killer
and he who thinks it killed,
both fail to understand;
it does not kill, nor is it killed.

It is not born,
it does not die;
having been,
it will never not be;
unborn, enduring,
constant, and primordial,
it is not killed
when the body is killed.

Arjuna, when a man knows the self
to be indestructible, enduring, unborn,
unchanging, how does he kill
or cause anyone to kill?

As a man discards
worn-out clothes
to put on new
and different ones,
so the embodied self
discards
its worn-out bodies
to take on other new ones.

Weapons do not cut it,
fire does not burn it,
waters do not wet it,
wind does not wither it.

It cannot be cut or burned;
it cannot be wet or withered;
it is enduring, all-pervasive,
fixed, immovable, and timeless.

It is called unmanifest,
inconceivable, and immutable;
since you know that to be so,
you should not grieve!

If you think of its birth
and death as ever-recurring,
then too, Great Warrior,
you have no cause to grieve!

Death is certain for anyone born,
and birth is certain for the dead;
since the cycle is inevitable,
you have no cause to grieve!

(*Bhagavad Gita* 2:18–27.)

1.

Candle

Barbed wire

Amnesty candle

(a) Look at picture of the candle. Write down your thoughts in a 'stream of consciousness' flow. Discuss the words and ideas that came into your head with your neighbour.

(b) Now do the same for the picture of the barbed wire, then the picture of the candle.

(c) Now write a 'haiku' (a three-line poem, the first line of 5 syllables, the second of 7 syllables and the third of 5 syllables) based on some of your ideas.

(d) Write another haiku, this time based on the reading of the chapter on Peace and Conflict.

2. As you read at the end of this chapter, there seem to be two different approaches to killing within the Hindu tradition.

(a) Read the two passages (a) and (b) on p. 49 very carefully.

(b) Summarise the main teachings of both in your own words.

(c) Write a short statement that you think would reflect a position in between these two approaches.

(d) Discuss with your neighbour your responses to the questions above. Then think about what it means to 'kill with a word or gesture'.

(e) You are preparing a four-minute speech for a debate in Parliament. Choose a partner to debate against. The topic is either *The soldier exists to kill* or *The line beyond which we kill is drawn by the individual*.

Choose one of these and, trying to use only material from this section, prepare a 'for' and 'against' speech between you. In a real debate, who would 'win'?

Research

1. Find out what are the most common 'engines of destruction' used by military powers in Europe. How much do countries spend on their defence? (You might like to contrast this with the amount spent on other areas such as Health or Education.) Write to the Ministry of Defence to find out their position. Write to some of the Peace movements in this country, to see how their ideas differ.

2. What is Amnesty International? What kind of work does the organisation do?

Dictionary words

| SATYAGRAHA AHIMSA HIMSA |
| NON-VIOLENT NON-COOPERATION |

Relations with Other Faiths

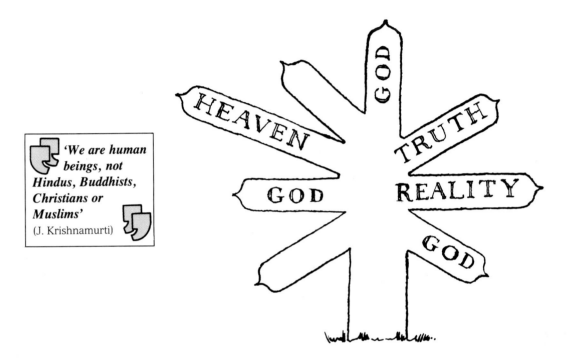

> 'We are human beings, not Hindus, Buddhists, Christians or Muslims'
> (J. Krishnamurti)

THE STRAIGHTEST PATH

According to ancient Hindu teaching, all religions are initiated by God, and aim at reaching God, but not all religions actually lead to God. Like rivers, the paths of different religions and different people flow in different ways. Some rivers take a straight route to the sea, others twist and curve in a circuitous route. So, the Hindu believes, some people genuinely want to find God, to achieve liberation, but others do not. For the Hindu, a straight path must be followed in order to reach the final stage of the journey to God: the Hindu tradition claims to present a straight path (**vidhi**) to its followers, but accepts that other religions may present a straight path too. Anyone who does not sincerely wish to find God is described as an **avidhisar** – one who does not take a prescribed straight path.

Although Hindus accept the truths of other religions, they claim that the Vedic religion is the highest form of truth which may be followed by anyone (although not taught by everyone). It is important to remember that Hindus do not usually speak of their religion as 'Hinduism', but as **sanatan dharma**, the eternal moral law. This law, or code, is not a dogmatic belief system, but provides truths that are valid for all people regardless of their religion. It is believed that *all* souls are constantly reborn until they reach the final stage of existence and are liberated from the round of life, death and rebirth. This is said to be an inescapable fact, like the heat from the sun.

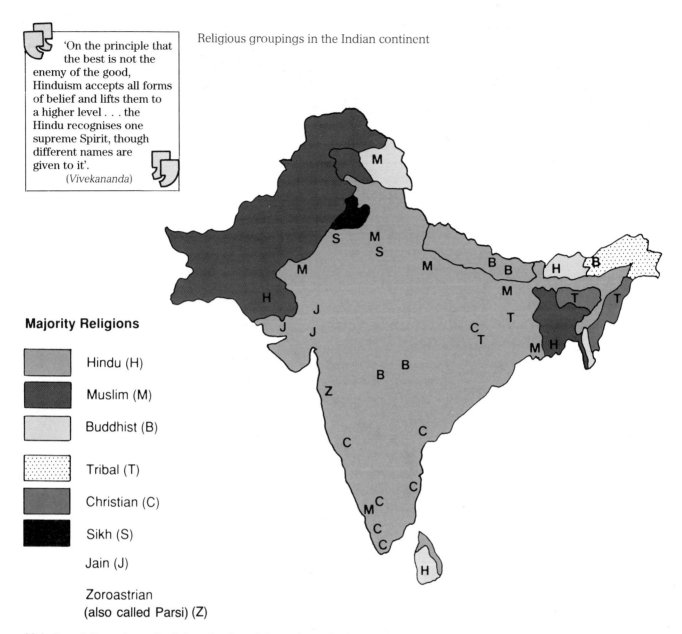

Religious groupings in the Indian continent

Majority Religions

Hindu (H)

Muslim (M)

Buddhist (B)

Tribal (T)

Christian (C)

Sikh (S)

Jain (J)

Zoroastrian
(also called Parsi) (Z)

Majority religions shown by tints, minority religions shown by letters

Because India is a multifaith country, where people of many religions live side by side, many Hindus develop an interest in and an awareness of the teachings of other religions, and are tolerant of people with different beliefs. Mahatma Gandhi describes his own early contact with the different branches of the Hindu tradition and with other religions in this way:

'In Rajkot . . . I got an early grounding in toleration for all branches of Hinduism and sister religions. For my father and mother would visit temples of different Hindu gods and would take or send us youngsters there. Jain monks also would pay frequent visits to my father, and would even go out of their way to accept food from us – non-Jains. They would have talks with my father on subjects religious and mundane.

He had, besides, Muslim and Parsi friends, who would talk to him about their own faiths and he would listen to them always with respect and often with interest. Being his nurse, I often had a chance to be present at these talks. These many things combined to inculcate in me a toleration for all faiths.' (*Autobiography*)

CONVERSION

Because of the attitude that all religions are acceptable if they lead to God, there was no tradition of conversion to Hinduism until recently. Most Hindus do not see the need for non-Hindus to convert; they believe that each religion meets the needs of an individual within his or her particular stage of development, or cultural background, and that one should use that particular path to find God.

Here is one Hindu's view of conversion:

> Conversion is change from one belief or dogma to another, from one ceremony to a more gratifying one, and it does not open the door to reality. On the contrary, gratification is a hindrance to reality. And yet that is what organised religions and religious groups are attempting to do; to convert you to a more reasonable or a less reasonable dogma, superstition or hope. They offer you a better cage. It may or may not be comfortable, depending on your temperament, but in any case it is a prison.
>
> You can be converted from one belief to another, from one dogma to another, but you cannot be converted to the understanding of reality. Belief is not reality. You can change your mind, your opinion, but truth or God is not a conviction: it is an experience not based on any belief or dogma, or on any previous experience.
>
> (J. Krishnamurti)

For Krishnamurti, the need to identify with one religious institution or other puts an end to all creative understanding, to all sense of self-discovery.

Activities

1. Here are some questions. Think about them carefully, then write your reply to each in the form of a letter. You may use quotations from this chapter.

   (a) *Dear Mrs Sharma,*
   I thought that you might be able to help me, since you are my son, Johnny's, science teacher. He has recently become very interested in Hindu meditation and yoga and spends hours in his room 'focusing his mind'. He used to be a very devout Christian, but has stopped going to Church altogether. Although I myself spend time in quiet prayer and reflection, I am worried that Johnny will lose his Christian faith, and be left with nothing solid, culturally or spiritually, to base his life on. Of course, I see his need to go on his own spiritual search, but feel that he should think twice before he converts to Hinduism, which is what he says he would like to do. What would you advise me to say to him?
   Yours sincerely
   Frank Rossi

   (b) *Dear Mr Gandhi,*
   At home I was brought up to believe that there was only one way to God, and that all other religions were not true. As a Hindu, what would your response be to that statement?
   Yours faithfully,
   Joan Gideon

2. Read the passage concerning Krishnamurti's attitude towards conversion.
   (a) In two sentences, define his attitude to organised religion.
   (b) Think about whether you agree with him. Now, in your own words, list the functions that organised religion has in this society (e.g. conducts rituals/important ceremonies marking the rites of passage, influences national laws). Next to each function, place a + or − sign to show whether you think it is helpful to the individual in his or her quest for religious understanding.

   Dictionary words

SANATAN DHARMA	VIDHI
AVIDHISAR	

RESOURCES LIST • RESOURCES LIST • RESOURCES LIST • RESOURCES LIST • RESOURCES LIST • RESOURCES LIST • RESOURCES LIST • RI

ES LIST • RESOURCES LIST • RESOURCES LIST • RESOURCES LIST • RESOURCES LIST • RESOURCES LIST • RESOURCES LIST • RESOURCES

Resources List

BAHREE, Patricia, *The Hindu World*, Macdonald, 1982

BOWEN, David G. (ed.), *Hinduism in England*, Bradford College, 1981

BURGHART, Richard (ed.), *Hinduism in Great Britain*, Tavistock, 1987

EMBREE, A.T. (ed.), *The Hindu Tradition*, Random House, New York, 1966

FISCHER, Louis, *The Life of Mahatma Gandhi*, Granada, 1982

GANDHI, M.K., *An Autobiography, or The Story of My Experiments with Truth*, Penguin Books edition, 1982

ISHERWOOD, C., *Ramakrishna and His Disciples*, Vedanta Press, California, 1965

JACKSON, R. and KILLINGLEY, D., *Approaches to Hinduism*, John Murray, 1988

KANITKAR, V.P. (Hemant), *We are Hindus*, St Andrew Press, 1987

KANITKAR, V.P., *Hindu Festivals and Sacraments*, 1984

KOLLER, J.M., *The Indian Way*, Collier Macmillan, 1982

O'FLAHERTY, W. Doniger (trans.), *The Rig Veda*, Penguin Books, 1987

KRISHNAMURTI, J., *Commentaries on Living*, 1st, 2nd, 3rd series, Theosophical Publishing House, 1956–73

SHARMA, Damodar, *Hindu Belief and Practice*, Edward Arnold, 1984

SHARMA, I.C. and DAUGERT, S.M., *Ethical Philosophies of India*, Johnson Publishing Co., Nebraska, 1965

SHARMA, Ursula, *Women's Work, Class and the Urban Household*, Tavistock, 1986

ZAEHNER, R.C., *Hindu Scriptures*, J.M. Dent, 1966.